klaus LEOPOLD

rethinking AGILE

Why Agile Teams Have Nothing To Do With Business Agility

www.LEANability.com

Rethinking Agile

December 2018

Text: Dolores Omann, Illustrations: Matthias Seifert, Graphic Design: Mario Simon-Hoor

Translation: Jennifer Minnich

Foto: Christian Kollarovits

ISBN 978-3-903205-39-0

Stay up to date

 rethinkingagile.com

 LEANability.com

 youtube.com/c/LeanBusinessAgility

 twitter.com/klausleopold

3

You can turn any problem into a mystery. There are now enough agile templates and frameworks to turn any simple insight into a challenge that naturally can only be resolved with this or that method or framework. Yes, I am sitting in a glass house. I make my money giving companies valuable tips and my name is associated with Kanban. However, my goal is to never make things more complicated than what they really are. And a simple insight goes along with this: An agile organization is not created by completely optimizing elements isolated from one another—in most cases this involves teams. Often, though, Agile odysseys start with this local (sub-)optimization, where at the same time their chosen agile method becomes the golden calf. Then the only attempt is to do the method justice rather than asking what creates more value for the customer. Typically, collaboration between the development areas of an organization and the business decision makers isn't taken into consideration.

In this book, combined with the power of illustration, I want to make a clear and meaningful point about this simple insight, which you can neither certify nor trademark. In the past two years, I have gone from conference to conference with my presentation "Why agile teams have nothing to do with business agility". Over and over, I receive feedback from people in the audience about how they have found themselves in the same trials and tribulations during agile transformations.

Do not expect this book to delve deep into theory. What you will read here is a general view of what goes wrong in many agile change projects and simple suggestions about how you can avoid these dead ends or correct your course. I do not present any solutions that are absolutely correct for every organization. Do not consider my wisdom the ultimate wisdom. Thinking for yourself is expressly permitted.

Agile odysseys often begin with local optimization

Hence, this book presumes a fundamental knowledge about agility and the mechanisms behind it. Perhaps your company has just started down the path of becoming agile, or you are already stuck knee-deep in the transformation and are asking yourself what the heck has gone wrong. In this case, you will probably find useful hints in this book. And perhaps while reading this book you will realize something that makes you smile to yourself, which means my goal has been achieved.

Enjoy!

KLAUS LEOPOLD

In the past few years, I have toured across many countries giving my talk on "Why agile teams have nothing to do with Business Agility". Over and over, I received so much positive feedback. Mostly I heard comments like, "This is exactly what happened to us!" So, I thought, "Maybe I should quickly make a book out of this!" But it didn't happen so quickly after all.

If you have seen my talks, you might have noticed that I am a fan of illustrative language. Books such as the illustrated version of "Reinventing Organizations" by Frederic Laloux and Etienne Appert fascinate me because the most important statements within the text are clearly and impressively reiterated through the illustrations. It was clear to me that the topic of business agility must be illustrated in order to express as boldly as possible the agile insanity that occasionally occurs in companies. And I wanted to publish it myself. However, I imagined it to be somewhat simpler than it was. I thought I only needed an illustrator and the book would be finished. So much for that theory.

In actuality, it became a mid-sized expedition to find the right illustrator. Which makes me even more pleased to have found Matthias Seifert. Although he had never dealt with this subject, he was able to understand the content quickly and translate it into pictures that kept the balance between the necessary earnestness and humor.

I would like to thank Dolores Omann one more time, who has assisted me since the first edition of "Kanban in der IT" (2012), for turning my ideas into readable text. Thanks also goes to Matthias Patzak for his intensive review of the book. It felt like he took time to consider every word in the text and gave fantastic input, which improved the quality of this book.

Text and pictures are naturally important components of an illustrated book, but without a stylish layout they remain just components. Mario Simon-Hoor took the individual pieces and made them into a whole, putting the finishing touch on this book.

Many thanks to Jennifer Minnich for the translation from German to English. She succeeded once again in translating not only the content, but also the spirit of the book, into English.
I would also like to thank Troy Magennis and Mike Freislich for providing valuable feedback on the English version.

114 pictures say more than 114,000 words

The cover of the book was a somewhat more difficult task and I needed several drafts until it felt and looked like I wanted. A heartfelt thank-you to my life and business partner, Katrin Dietze, for the wonderful book cover and for the never-ending patience she is always willing to give me.

KLAUS LEOPOLD

PART 1

The Problem
"We want agility!"

This is about a company that wanted to be **prepared** for the **future** and paved the way there with **good intentions.**

DEPENDENCIES
PROCESSES
CULTURE
TIME TO MARKET
ABILITY TO DELIVER
STRATEGIC NEGOTIATING
COORDINATION

Actually, nothing could go wrong. Upper management was committed, the budgets were available, the agile coaches were booked. In the last few months, there had been a realization within the company: "Others are quicker." It became clear to them that things could no longer go on like this. They would either finally improve their capacity to deliver, or the company would sooner or later disappear from the market.

There was never a shortage of good ideas and possibilities to pursue for the core business; quite the opposite. It was taking so much time to implement good ideas that the competition was already two steps ahead with a similar product, although these younger and more dynamic rivals had not reached the same level of market penetration. Unfortunately, the company had become a follower over the last few years, leading to difficulty even in its day-to-day business. The company could no longer rely on their once strong position as a market leader. Alternatives showed up in the market, the number of customers stagnated—and in some months even fell.

Something needed to change, that much was clear. And management quickly figured out what needed to improve:

- The **Time-to-Market** should be optimized.

- Using **fast customer feedback,** necessary changes should be recognized and integrated earlier. That means: The customer must be significantly more involved in the development process than they had been till now.

- The company should be **ready for the future.** Digitalization, the Internet of Things, machine learning and crypto currencies were only a few of the buzz words that kept coming up in the discussions. But there would be no future company if they continued operating so rigidly in the market.

Recently, management had heard about companies with similar problems. In all of the case studies and whitepapers, Scrum, Kanban, Design Thinking, SAFe®, mOre or LeSS and other miracle practices were being talked about, all of which promised massive improvements for the problem at hand. That was the solution:

We will make our business agile!

TRANSFORMATION PREPARATIONS – EXEMPLARY

600 IT employees were encouraged to use agile methods in order to get the business back on track. The project initiators carefully examined the fundamentals of various agile methods and took part in corresponding training and certifications. This much was clear to them: "We cannot simply force a new method on the organization—that is not the point. What's important to us is allowing agile principles and values to have a greater role in our corporate culture and to actually put these principles to practice." To achieve this, the head of internal organizational development was given a mandate to implement an 18-month **transformation project.**

I actually find this extremely funny: "We are going to implement a waterfall project to become agile." But don't let me get ahead of the story.

The departments and teams could even choose the agile framework they wanted to use. However, management established some parameters that everyone needed to follow—because the project initiators promised the greatest leveraging effect based on these **conditions:**

1. All teams should be **cross-functional.** In doing this, the initiators wanted to eliminate any existing dependencies to reduce coordination effort and waiting time, thus improving Time-to-Market. To deliver a product, product development teams in which all competencies are represented would replace what was, until now, teams organized according to specialized disciplines.

A fundamentally good idea! It is advantageous if you are able to bundle together as many competencies as possible.

2. Every team should be organized according to the premise: **One team, one product.**

This is also a good idea. For one, this approach helps to reduce dependencies. Not to mention that in most organizations, specialized teams work on several products and projects at the same time and are rarely able to concentrate working on one item. That costs time.

3. Even if the teams could choose the agile method they wanted to use, the following **minimum requirements** needed to be fulfilled:

a. The work should be visible, i.e. it should be **visually managed**

b. Every team was compelled to hold **daily Standups** in front of the boards.

c. Regular **Retrospectives** should provide the teams a perspective on possibilities for improvement.

d. **Two measurements** should be established as an additional feedback mechanism for the teams and the transformation. Not to define quantitative goals, but to have further reference points for assessing the effect of the measures and improvements being implemented. The following measures would help with this:

● **Throughput:** The number of work items that are completed in a given timeframe (such as projects per month, Stories per Sprint, etc.). In Scrum, this is referred to as **Velocity.**

● **Cycle Time:** This indicates how fast work is completed.

I found this practical approach towards selecting the agile methods very **forward-thinking.** Not every method is appropriate for every context and every method can fail if implemented poorly. However, the most prominent part of agile methods, visualizing work and working methods, always makes sense: Everyone in a company should be able to see what a team, department or other organizational unit is currently working on and where the problems lie. It's smart to connect this visual management with daily Standups because fast feedback loops allow for quicker responses and appropriate coordination to apparent changes or customer wishes.

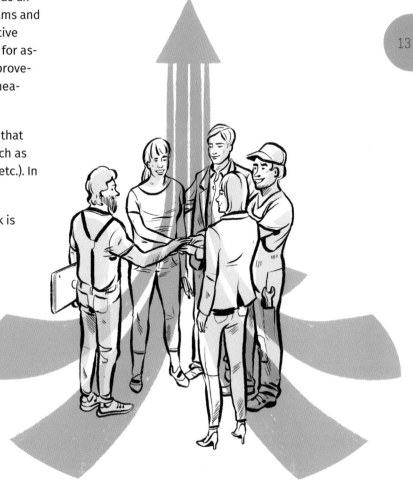

It is also important to take a step back from the operational work on a regular basis, which is what a team does in a Retrospective. A Retrospective is used to contemplate what can be done differently or better in the future. If you continuously do what you've always done, the probability is very high that the result will continue to be the same. Where measurements are concerned: fantastic! But despite the enthusiasm about the changes requiring a human component to make a company agile, the economic purpose of delivering a better product more quickly is often forgotten. This is even more critical these days because what gets talked about often counts more than what gets achieved.

14

What is a Standup?

Standups are short meetings that occur frequently—daily, for example—while standing before a task board or Kanban board. Within a maximum 15-minute timeframe, the group discusses what needs to be done to complete the work, how impediments and quality issues will be dealt with and who should work on what. The focus is on the work, not on the individual members in the group.

What is a Retrospective?

The goal of a Retrospective is to perform a collaborative review of how work was executed over a given timeframe and infer improvements from this review. Operational work is intentionally exposed in order to observe, from a meta-level, the working methods, processes, effects of previous improvements, feedback from customers and colleagues, as well as the team's morale. Although the Retrospective is the core of improvement, it is often neglected because of poor execution [Leanability E020, 2017].

THE TRANSFORMATION PROCESS

Even as an extremely skeptical observer, I must say: Hats off! Behind the buzzwords "agile transformation", there was a palpable genuine effort towards improving outcomes and thinking about things differently. Agile organizations often call themselves such because in some corner of the company somewhere there is a team using Scrum. In this company, however, the changes went to the core, and they tried to reconstruct a large portion of the organization according to agile principles. At the same time, method choice was left to the teams themselves—depending on what the employees found appropriate for their area of responsibility. I cried agile tears of joy at such an approach. So, how was the transformation actually carried out?

Please Note: During implementation, the following steps were interwoven with one another and, as such, were not completed sequentially.

TRAINING

All 600 IT employees had the pleasure of taking part in a one-day basic training which focused on **"agile mindset"**. Anyone who has dealt with Agile and agile practices has often heard and perhaps even internalized this idea: The agile methods themselves are not the driving factors for success, rather the mindset behind them determines their effectiveness. Basically, I agree with this. However, you cannot simply implant a new mindset because the project plan says so. Establish mindset, done! **It doesn't work that way.**

I don't believe that you can change a collective mindset with a one-day basic training. Nonetheless, it takes a certain amount of effort to drag 600 employees, along with management, through such a training. The only positive effect from such an undertaking is on the bank account of the consulting company providing the training.

You can probably pick up on a bit of sarcasm on my part—because I am being sarcastic.

15

REORGANIZATION THROUGH SELF-ORGANIZATION

The company realigned the cross-functional teams according the product structure. Management did not go about this arbitrarily, i.e. the employees were not simply assigned to individual teams. Management only decided which teams were needed for which products. So, instead of teams being assigned from above, a **marketplace** was organized. Over two days, team leaders used display booths to advertise their team and the available jobs. A budget was assigned to each team ahead of time—based on the strategic focus—so they could "buy" the necessary employees. The employees were allowed to decide in which team they wanted to work. In my opinion, this was a pretty cool approach.

At the marketplace, the team already discussed and often had decided on the agile practices they wanted to use. After the teams had formed, team members then took part in the necessary training. For example, there were Scrum Master and Product Owner trainings, and if a team had decided to use Kanban, they could visualize their initial workflow in a system design workshop and at the same time consolidate the team.

EXTERNAL SUPPORT

Reorganizing **600 people** is an ambitious program. In a short period of time, the people in this company were supposed to do—sometimes in completely new roles—something that they have never done before. The company hired **16 external Agile coaches** to execute the needed training, provide an outsider's perspective on implementing the agile methods and help the teams practice using these methods. At first glance this might seem like a lot, but it is realistic when put in context to the ambitious dimension of the undertaking. This makes sense in my opinion because often when changes are made, new working methods are used only as long as the consultants are in house. Based on the amount of money this company was spending on the transformation, this is exactly the effect they did not want.

17

What is a System Design workshop?

The visible end product of a System Design workshop is a Kanban board. The visualization itself is helpful, but it is not essential, even if that sounds somewhat strange. The most important objective in such a workshop is to gain a mutual understanding about how a group of people are currently working together. The visualization does not represent a desired or dictated process, rather it represents what is actually being done right now. This current Kanban system is the starting point for improvements. That's why it is so important that a Kanban system is designed by those who are using it.

THE RESULTS AFTER TWELVE MONTHS

To implement the minimum requirements—creating cross-functional product teams, visualization, Standups, Retrospectives and measurements—the company set an **eighteen-month timeframe.** The transformation itself was set up as a project within the organization. Under the guidance of a Transition Manager, the Transition Team planned exactly when which milestones of the Agile rollout should be achieved using which measures. The project "Agile Business" was established and rolled out.

After twelve months had passed, the initiators of the agile transformation wanted to evaluate the project's progress, so they did an interim **review of the project.** The plan seemed to be working:

- **More than 80 percent** of the teams were "fully transformed" (directly quoted from the Transition Manager) and fulfilled the stipulated framework conditions. They were cross-functionally staffed, made their work—depending on the method—transparent on the boards, held Standups and searched for improvement possibilities in regular Retrospectives.

● **It was important** for the Transition Team to know about the employee morale in order to take corrective measures in the case that it was suffering. Every six months an employee survey was conducted and the most current survey showed that communication and coordination had qualitatively improved. The teams kept each other up to date on the status of their work, and they knew who was doing what and who was responsible for what.

Overall, the mood was positive. The majority of the teams had held to the initial transformation requirements and visualizing the work was found to be very helpful. Some employees were not able to adapt to the new transparency and left the company. But that was to be expected, change is often hard for some people.

But for the most part, it was going well. Wasn't it?

SHOW US YOUR NUMBERS

Implementing metrics was one of the framework conditions of the agile transition that were placed on the teams. The Transition Team took a look at how the **cycle time** and the **throughput** had progressed at the team and project level—and weren't any smarter for it. Certain patterns showed up over and over again, so the Transition Team took representative measurements in order to better understand what was going on. For example, let's look at the progression of the throughput for the Scrum teams and the changes in cycle time for the Kanban teams. Afterwards, we will see whether or not the projects were getting completed more quickly.

THROUGHPUT TREND OF THE SCRUM TEAMS

The Transition Team first looked at how **velocity** changed in the Scrum teams.

In every Sprint, a Scrum team makes a commitment to complete a certain amount of work (in Scrum-speak we would be talking about the number of User Stories or Story Points). At the end of each Sprint, the amount of committed work is compared to what actually gets delivered—this result is recorded on the y-axis (Number of Story Points). This gives us the velocity—the speed, or throughput, of a team in a given timeframe.

20

The diagram shows the aggregated velocity of the Scrum teams within the company. The dotted line represents the results that were expected. When everything is running smoothly in a Scrum team, the velocity should continuously increase. The expectations of increased speed were fairly low at the beginning: The team needed to establish themselves first and get used to the new working methods. However, after this initial training period, the curve should sharply increase and eventually level out, but still continue in an upwards direction. If Retrospec-

tives are also held and continuous improvements made, the line should steadily continue upwards and never turn downwards.

Nonetheless, the **actual trend** of the Scrum teams looked completely different. The teams managed to get off to a good start and velocity increased sharply. Then all of a sudden, the line flattened out and was now in a downward trend. The performance had strongly diminished over time.

CYCLE TIME TREND OF THE KANBAN TEAMS

Next, the Transition Team took a closer look at the **cycle time of the Kanban teams.** At the team level, the cycle time is fairly easy to determine: For each completed piece of work, the time difference between the start date and completion date is calculated. Ideally, the cycle times become shorter over time.

If the **cycle times** from several teams are aggregated, a good pattern will show the trendline going down over time. Just as we saw with the throughput progression expectations, you would typically expect a slight increase in the cycle time to start with because the teams must get used to their new working methods. Afterwards, however, the line should quickly trend downwards. This indicates that teams are finishing work more quickly as time goes on, thus decreasing the cycle time. This is exactly what gets advertised with Agile working methods. Scrum

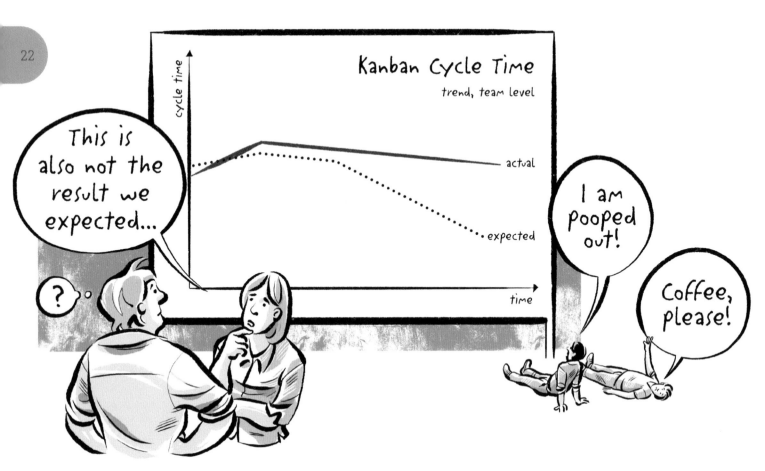

consultants promise that you can deliver more work more quickly. Kanban consultants promise that the cycle time at the very least will be **cut in half,** and you can actually expect more than that.

It looked quite different for the Kanban teams in this company. As expected, the cycle time increased slightly at the beginning but only marginally decreased over time. The line followed a downward trend, but the improvement did not even reach the 1 percent mark—a cycle time reduced by half was nowhere to be found.

Regardless, whether **Scrum or Kanban**—it was clear that ability of the teams to deliver had not changed much. And let's remember: "Quicker Time-to-Market" was the goal of the agile transformation.

What is the velocity?

In Scrum, velocity is the measure of team's throughput. It shows how much functionality a team can deliver in a Sprint. The amount that can be delivered is measured in Story Points.

What is a User Story?

A User Story is used to formulate a requirement, for example on a piece of software to be developed. In the Agile world, a simple format has been established:

As a **<type of user>,**
I want **<some goal or objective>**
so that **<benefit, value>.**

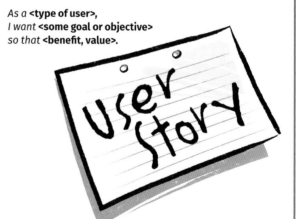

What are Story Points?

Story Points represent the complexity of a User Story, not the time required. When estimating several Stories, the complexity of the Stories are determined in relation to one another.

23

PROJECTS ARE NOT BEING COMPLETED MORE QUICKLY

The analysis of the team metrics was anything but exhilarating for the Transition Team. It was also problematic that comparison values were missing. It was difficult to judge whether the agile transformation had a positive effect because there were no "baseline" measurements from before the transformation. Since the teams were completely reorganized as part of the transformation, it wasn't really possible to determine if, for example, the performance of the Scrum teams had improved or deteriorated.

The company did however have metrics which could be used to compare the performance before and after the agile initiative: the **project cycle time.** This is an especially important metric because the organization's goal was to reduce the project cycle time and shorten the Time-to-Market. There were projects before the transition and projects after the agile transition, although after the transition projects were given the more agile name "initiatives". Thus, comparative data was available.

In this diagram, we see three types of lines: the thicker line on the left side mirrors the time before the agile transformation. Because the Time-to-Market was steadily increasing—what you can see in the upward movement of the thick line—the company decided to do something about it. It was clear to everyone involved that this line would not immediately move downwards, but rather would increase slightly after the transformation got started because of the changes being implemented. But, based on all the efforts undertaken, such as training and coaching support, you would expect the Time-to-Market to drastically reduce once the new working methods were being used.

And again, the opposite happened. Yes, the Time-to-Market had continued to deteriorate at the start of the reorganization. However, it continued to deteriorate... put another way: Projects were now being delivered more slowly than in the pre-Agile times. That was simply a catastrophe.

A huge pile of money had been put into this **agile transformation.** The management and the Transition Team had put a lot of thought into how best to achieve it. Management made the big decision to set up cross-functional teams and organize them according to product lines. Professionals supported the transformation and trained internal coaches. 600 people learned how to work with Scrum, Kanban, Standups, Retrospectives and metrics.

And now the overall goal—being able to react more quickly to market needs—had not been achieved and was in fact further away than before. A transformation that took the company **from bad to worse?**

25

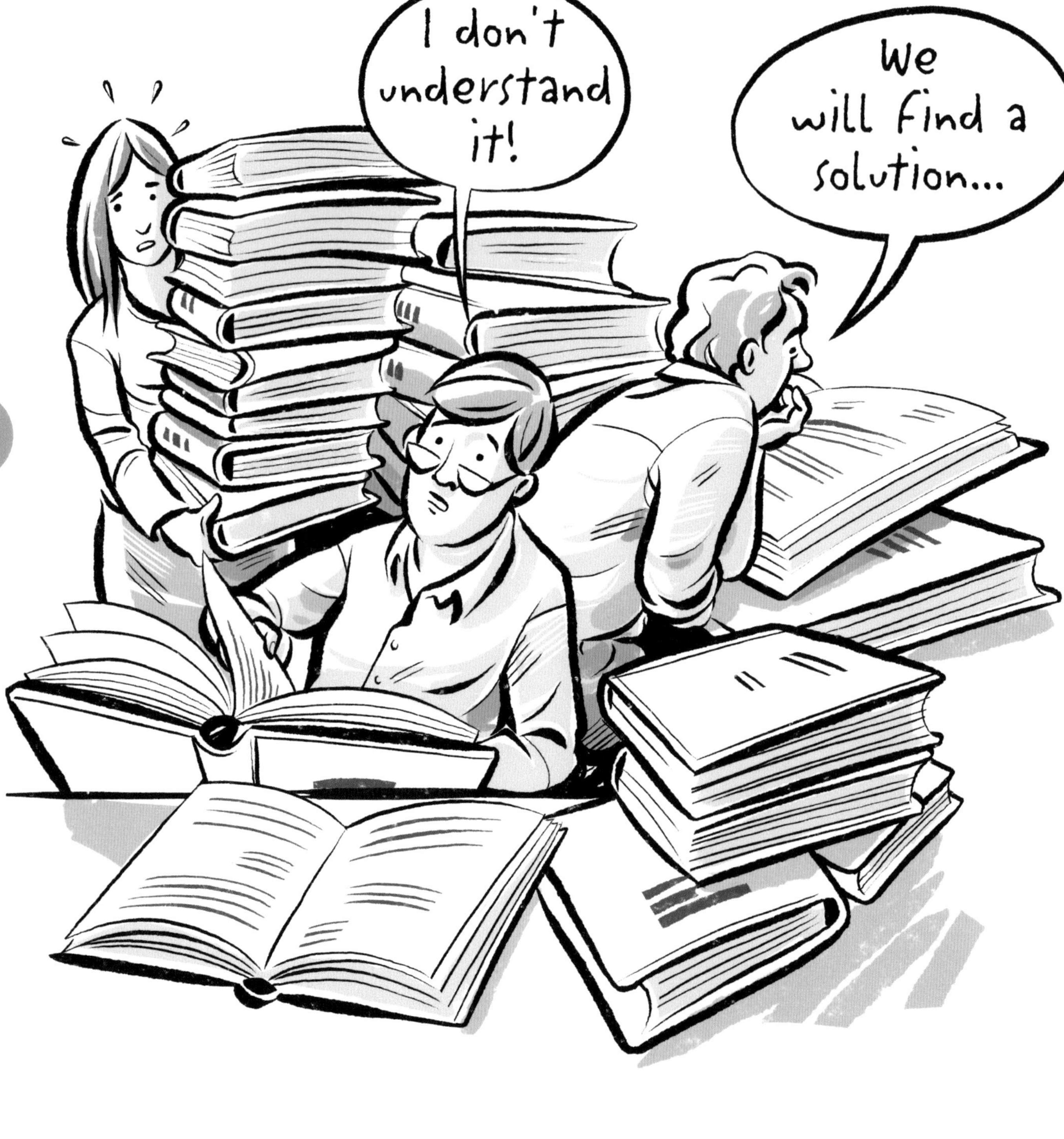
I don't understand it!
We will find a solution...

WHAT THE @$*# WAS THE PROBLEM HERE?

PART 2

The Causes

Looking for Stumbling Blocks

29

About inferring things simplistically, hidden dependencies, a burgeoning value stream and the power of **WIP limits.**

I read your book and kind of have an idea what the causes for our situation might be", said the lady on the telephone. In "Practical Kanban" [Leopold, 2016], I made my displeasure with the Agile world known because I came across the same outlandish viewpoints over and over again. Namely, that the success of an agile company occurs by simply compelling all the teams to use an agile method of their choosing. Multiplying the methods then creates something extremely new and fast.

Nobody looks at the overall value stream because the teams will straighten things out. And while the teams devotedly place **WIP limits** on their work, everything remains the same at the portfolio level. It's actually worse than that: Since the teams are agile as of deadline X, even **more projects** get started because now everything goes quicker because we are agile. Diligent cross-functional teams try to defend their WIP limits on Stories and tasks while being smothered in projects at the same time. And because very few of those responsible for agile transformations are aware of this beforehand, I receive calls every day from people who are standing in front of the shards of their efforts asking themselves what happened.

So, now an employee of the Transition Team of this company contacted me. They were so hopeful when starting the transition of the **600 IT colleagues** to agile and couldn't figure out why the **Time-to-Market** wasn't improving. The slight tone of despair was hard to ignore while she was telling her story because she had personally put a lot of effort into the transition. She read through numerous books and blogs about agility, she completed Scrum and Kanban training and kept herself up-to-date. The way she and her colleagues took on this agile transformation sounded very professional and well though-out to me. Nevertheless, she was at the end of her rope given the results of the transformation.

She asked me to come on location to see the situation and then hold a workshop to work through the assumptions and viewpoints of the **decision makers**—because making the IT agile was a request from the highest level. What did the managers imagine an agile business to be when they started working towards this goal? In their understanding, what was necessary to achieve this goal? Behind their good intentions, was there a solid understanding about the interrelationships in the value stream, or did they just blindly hop on the Agile bandwagon? Afterwards, I requested to be shown the **work and metrics** from several teams in order to find out what underlying assumptions were used as they approached their agile transformation.

CAUSE #1: THE PITFALL OF SIMPLISTIC INFERENCE IN THE CHANGE PROCESS

What did they want to achieve in this company: an optimized **Time-to-Market**, faster customer **feedback** and a fresh **mindset**—accompanied by a structure that would be prepared to meet the challenges of the future. Nowadays, companies and the people in them rarely have the open and **unbiased enthusiasm** of Gimli. In the film "Lord of the Rings: The Return of the King", the dwarf warrior says: "Certainty of death. Small chance of success. What are we waiting for?!"

When a company wants to change, the people within the company want to know what the result will be and how they will get there. So, they search for assurances, and plans give them this assurance. Having a plan is a good thing. It only becomes problematic if the decision makers are drawn towards simplistic inferences or reach for blueprints, which have become plentiful in the Agile scene.

During my discussions with the company management, I recognized that they had also been **inferring things too simplistically.**

1st Inference: We must become agile in order to reach this goal. Yes, of course! That means we must start an agile transformation for our 600 IT employees. But how do we go about this?

2nd Inference: We need agile teams using agile methods that are extremely fast and agile at delivering our products. We need Scrum Masters, Product Owners, Agile Coaches, Service Delivery Managers, Business Owners, and and and. finally, we need a proper reorganization and then everything will definitely be better. But how should the tasks and responsibilities be combined in these new roles?

3rd Inference: We need to define which roles are allowed to do what, who must sit in which meeting with whom, how often these meetings need to occur in order to be effective, and so on.

This organization made a **wrong turn** early on in their thought process and along the way had confused the **means for the purpose**. At the very beginning, it was going about improving their Time-to-Market—now, however, everyone was talking about stupid rules that were written down years ago in some kind of agile framework.

And this happens quite often: As soon as management decides that Daily standups, Retros, cross-functional teams, etc., are the requirements for achieving their goal, implementing these agile working methods becomes the goal itself. The focus—for the teams as well as for management—is placed on whether or not all of the methods' rules are being followed correctly. **Agility** is reduced to something that it shouldn't be: a **method**. Because then it no longer goes about what the **company** gains from it, not to mention the **customer**, who falls completely into the background.

What is the result after these inferences have been made? The entire organization talked about the most exciting questions, such as "Can the Product Owner take part in a Retrospective?" or "Is the Scrum Master also allowed to do work operatively in the team?" It was also easy to argue over **isolated opinions:** "We definitely won't use Scrum because then we must work with Timeboxes" vs. "We definitely won't use **Kanban** because it doesn't have Timeboxes".

Often during such discussions, I'll have a perplexed look on my face and think to myself: "Huh?!?! What in the world does that have to do with the **goals** you want to achieve?"

33

THE CHANGE PROCESS AS A "PROJECT"

Before the workshop, several of the managers greeted me as "Klaus, the one who is going to help us with our agile project". They explained their approach towards the agile project and how it seemed to be bearing fruit, especially in terms of employee satisfaction, but that now the agile project was in a precarious state.

Project — I had an idea what was happening here. After reorganizing, something completely different should have been created: something flexible, adaptable, something amazing! That's why it's best to plan your change process according to the established company-internal project management methods? As if transformation simply moves from one state to the next—especially from one "mindset" into the next—according to the due dates on a calendar. What I have seen happen in many organizations also happened in this company: Although agility

lives from the **pull principle**, they tried to jumpstart the project using a **push principle**—"make it your project" as the home-improvement store advertisement goes. The teams involved were able to select the method they wanted to work with, so a bit of pull principle was present. However, the entire transformation process was set up as a **waterfall project** with **milestones** and **checklists**. I like to stay away from dogma, but I have had the best experiences with the following approach:

> If the desired state is agility, the way there should already be agile.

35

Pull Principle vs. Push Principle

Agile working methods have copied a considerable amount from the Toyota Production System (TPS). An essential mechanism for controlling the workflow is the **Pull Principle:** A teams only picks up the next piece of work from the previous stage when they have available capacity, i.e. other work has been completed and their WIP limit will not exceeded (we'll get to the WIP limits a bit later). In a traditional working environment, though, finished work is simply pushed along into the next processing step **(Push Principle** or "throw it over the fence").

CHANGE IS A NEW ORGANIGRAM — MIXING UP CAUSE AND EFFECT

As just stated, people need something to hold on to in times of change. They want to see what the new will look like because it gives them the illusion of **oversight and predictability,** i.e. security. The most tangible item in a re-organization is always the new organigram, which is why so many managers hold on so tightly to it. This means the **setup**, rather than the **processes**, become the focus of the change or improvement.

Apparently, an **agile organigram** is created when you simply toss the employees up in the air, put new labels on them and allow them to land at a different location in the organization. And grouped into cross-functional teams as neatly as possible, who naturally sit together in one room—obviously. If Herbert sits next to Hubert and Maria next to Brigitte, then everything will be ok. Then it will work!

Unfortunately, there are now a number of **ready-made organizational models** that attempt to show management how it is done. In the case of **Spotify,** it was not their intention to deliver a template to many companies across the globe. Spotify made the mistake in 2012 of

talking about their internal organization that made sense for the goals they were trying to achieve at that time [Leanability E020, 2017]. The setup of this more or less "temporary" organization and, above all, the cool organizational unit names like **Tribes, Chapters and Guild** stuck in people's heads. The **Spotify model** was a striking example of how an innovative agile organization could be set up, fulfilling a desire of those who wanted to be able to copy their success.

Except Spotify doesn't consider its organizational structure to be the secret of its success, but rather as something extremely transient or even somewhat negligible. The **organizational model** does not make Spotify agile; Spotify **is** agile and thus chose that organizational structure for a time in order to overcome specific challenges—today their organizational structure looks different. Cliff Hazel, Agile Coach Chapter Lead at Spotify (cool title, please copy it immediately!), paraphrased W. Edwards Deming one time during a talk with me [The Deming Institute, 2018]: "Every organization is set up perfectly for the results they deliver." So, if an organization had the exact same problem as Spotify did in 2012, then their model might be recommended. But perhaps not. Success depends on answering one question: **How** do we make our money and **which problem** are we trying to solve?

Basically, the customer doesn't really care whether Mr. Meier is sitting in office 238 or 145 and is participating in the Guild or not. As a Netflix customer, for example, I could care less which programmers are sitting next to each other and which hip titles they have. "WANT TO WATCH A FILM" is the only thing that interests me as a customer. What does interest me a bit more are the processes at Netflix, which are hopefully set up so that I can watch the film whenever I want without issue. Surprisingly, the Netflix employees' salaries are not paid by Netflix, but rather from the customers that use Netflix. In many companies, however, the customer doesn't appear anywhere in the organigrams.

If instead you place the **focus** on the **organizational processes** and permanently optimize it to fulfill the **customers' needs,** it's possible that at some point the organizational structure will change. But then the structure is oriented towards necessities and current insights, not on wishes. **"Agile"** is what the organization becomes through its own development, not something that goes live according to a particular deadline.

37

> **Organizational change should start with the organizational processes because fulfilling customer wishes, as well as the Time-to-Market, is a question of the processes used, collaboration and dependencies.**

CAUSE #2: DEALING WITH DEPENDENCIES BETWEEN TEAMS AND PRODUCTS

After I had checked out the **management situation** and came to the first realizations, I continued on to the **teams.** I found it amazing in this company: All teams had made—as was required by the framework conditions—their work visible. It didn't matter which team I visited: There was either a Kanban wallpaper, a Scrum board or some other type of visualization. That made it easier for me to have discussions with the teams about their work. We didn't discuss abstract processes and instead discussed the boards, which reflected their working methods. It was noticeable from both management and the teams that they wanted to turn things around for the better. At the point when I came to this company, more than 80 percent of the teams were already working with their chosen methods—thus, we could have good, concrete discussion at the boards.

Very often I saw **boards** that were constructed like this: I noticed an area on boards everywhere:

"**External Waiting**". Every team had visualized this area differently—sometimes as a parking space, some with just a blocker sticker—but always with the indication that a team could not work further on that task. They were waiting on deliveries, information or on services, such as opening ports in the firewall or making changes to database fields in a different product. In many cases it meant that the process must continue on another board within the organization since it wasn't just dealing with dependencies on external deliverers.

I went looking for **patterns** and asked questions like: "Which teams do you often have to wait for?" and "With which team do you have the most interactions where you regularly are waiting on something?" My goal was to make these interactions visible in **dependency graphs,** and so I worked through from team to team consolidating the fractals. Gradually a picture started to form and it was clear which teams were being utilized quite often.

Personally, I find **dependency graphs** fascinating, but the management and teams were mostly shocked at first. Their idea was to eliminate as many dependencies as possible. That's why teams were newly arranged as cross-functional teams where each one was only working on one product. The teams shouldn't even have to wait on other teams. And yet there were a number of **dependencies** visible that naturally increased the **cycle times.** Because what goes out of one system must first be prioritized in the next system. For example, if the work lands at a Scrum team, it must wait at least one Sprint until it gets processed.

WHAT DID THEY FORGET TO CONSIDER?

1. **One product, many teams.** It was correct that each team, in most cases, only worked on one product. However, several teams were often needed for one product. This created dependencies between the teams working on the same product.

2. **Dependencies between products.** The products themselves weren't completely independent from one another. When a change was made in Product 1, something also needed to be changed in Product 2. And when something in Product 2 was altered, something in Product 7 also needed a change.

3. **Peculiarities in knowledge work.** We're talking about 600 people in IT here. In so-called knowledge work, I don't know any organization with more than 30 employees that has absolutely no dependencies and a single team generating 100 percent value for the customer. Usually, several teams are involved in the delivery of a product in one way or another.

You can eliminate dependencies between teams and departments **as much as possible** if, for example, you offer completely identical products or services. This is possible at Buurtzorg, the health care company that Frederic Laloux wrote about in "Reinventing Organizations" [Laloux 2016], which has become the **prime example of self-organization.** Each team offers the same services, but there can be variations if caregivers decide to personalize the care services they offer. But even at Buurtzorg, necessary connections—**dependencies**—exist beyond just the daily work, such as the administrative units of the organization. Just as in every other organization, there are marketing, sales or legal departments—not every company can afford to put an attorney in every team. Not to mention that certain matters affecting the entire organization need to be dealt with centrally and not in the individual teams.

The idea of eliminating all dependencies in an organization is **not realistic.** An organization is not a container for completely independent teams—at least not in knowledge work.

There should be as many dependencies eliminated as possible. Most important, though, is good management of every dependency which remains.

40

41

> And therefore, the performance of the whole is never the sum of the parts taken separately, but it's the product of their interactions.
>
> Russel L. Ackoff

THE FASTEST F IN THE WORLD
OR
HOW YOU SUB-OPTIMIZE SYSTEMS

Yes, I know, I'm repeating myself. If you have read one of my other books or heard one of my talks, you know this quote from Russell Ackoff well. The thing is, **it's simply true.**

As we have just seen, despite all of the **cross-functional** and teams-for-products separation efforts in this company, many **acute dependencies** still existed. The situation did not improve when the teams started using agile methods. A team might phenomenally increase their performance and continuously improve themselves, but the effect of this local improvement is limited to the team itself.

Stringing together locally optimized units does **not** create a globally optimized system—as much as I hate to say it. Quite the opposite: If a team optimizes itself to the highest degree, the entire value chain can get messed up. Instead, the whole point is to create a value chain that is oriented towards the customers' wishes.

Let's look at the problem using a **keyboard.** We'll assume that the 600 IT employees in this company offer **correspondence letters** as their product. Each **team** is responsible for exactly **one** letter of the alphabet.

What is the principle of correspondence? Certainly not a random concatenation of letters in the alphabet. We want our correspondence to have meaningful words used to create meaningful sentences that ultimately create a meaningful text. That is the customer's requirement. And it is **completely irrelevant how quickly** the individual keys on the keyboard are struck.

The same thing happens in a company: If every team operates exactly one key, **it doesn't matter how quickly** an individual team works. Even if we have the fastest "F"-team on the planet in our organization, a team so fast that smoke rises up from the keyboard, the correspondence will not be finished more quickly because of it.

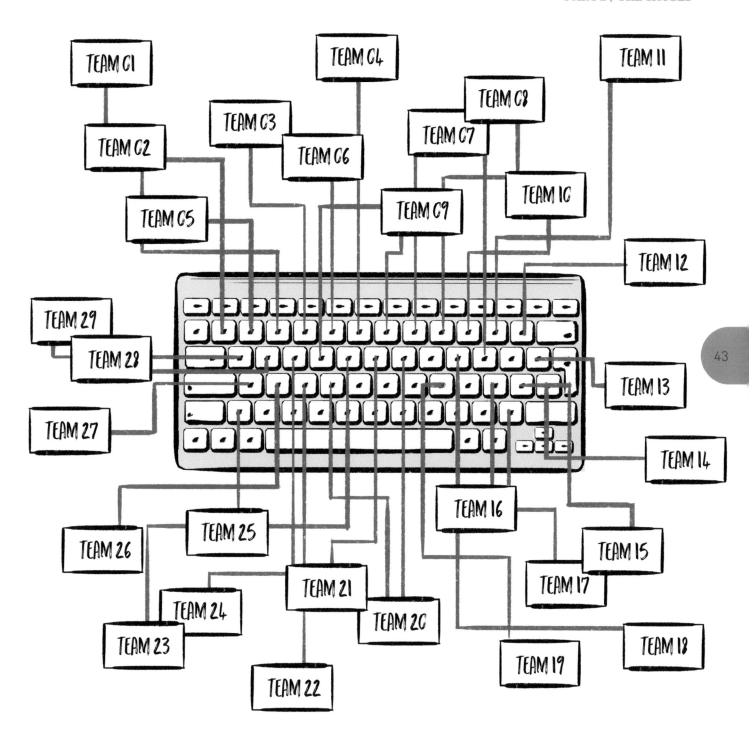

43

Thus, it isn't important how fast individual teams within an organization work. If we want to increase the **system output,** we must ensure that the right team is working on the **right thing** at the right time. Put another way: It's about the dependencies, or better said, how you deal with them.

This company still had it pretty good. For the most part, several teams worked on one product and very few worked on more than one product. The opposite is often the reality in many companies, though. There are many products and many teams — one team works on many products, and one product needs many teams to move things along.

The call for **high-performance teams** gives me a headache when I see that nobody is thinking about the **process.** An organization's agility is not created by stringing together a bunch of agile teams. Agility is created when the **inter-actions** between teams are agile.

CAUSE #3:
AN INCOMPLETE VALUE
STREAM

So, we had found out that there were many more **dependencies** than anyone thought and that they were not being **managed**. Something puzzled me the entire time I was standing in front of the team boards: **The boards were fairly short.** If I had been visiting a five-man operation, it might have been understandable. Naturally, we're not focusing on who has the longest...process. In this case, however, such short and simple processes, along with a short value creation stream, seemed quite improbable. Here were teams of between 7 and 14 people working in an IT department with 600 employees in a company that was twice as large as the department itself.

"**Okay, so you are** in development", I commenced with my questioning. "When you have finished development, then everything is completely finished and value for the customer has been generated?" At first, everyone nodded vigorously, some even let out an emphatic "Yes, of course!". After a moment of reflection, though, another person tentatively raised their voice: "Well, more precisely, **integration** comes afterwards."

45

Good to know! Together we modeled integration as part of the value creation illustration, so the board now looked like this:

"But after integration, everything is finished?", I continued to ask. The team members gave themselves a moment to think before they answered. "Actually, after integration comes business department acceptance." The board grew another step with the **acceptance tests.**

Gradually, the team got used to the idea that this board was going to be somewhat longer. I didn't even need to ask about the next step. "After that, we of course need to do a **release**", was immediately thrown at me.

Now I hit the brakes for a moment. With **"Integration", "Acceptance Testing" and "Release",** we had three steps visualized on the board that could have a substantial impact on the Time-to-Market. For this reason, I wanted to look at the steps more closely and asked, "At what intervals is integration done? And how often are acceptance tests performed and how often are there releases?" The core of the puzzle began to reveal itself. Integration was in a relatively timely manner, namely monthly. However, the acceptance testing as well as the releases were only done **four times a year.** This is extremely useful information when it's going about improving the Time-to-Market. **How** should you get to the market faster like this?

WHERE THERE IS A FLOW, THERE IS ALSO A SOURCE

All right, we had worked through the **downstream** to some extent. If there is a downstream, there is often also an upstream. Before development can even start, presumably some decisions need to be made. I packaged this in the (not so subtle) question: "At the beginning of the board stands the Backlog. So, you just simply start and nothing happens beforehand?" Of course, that wasn't the case. "No, you can't really say that it starts here. The Backlog is just the starting point for development." That's a good piece of information, so we renamed the Backlog **"Development Backlog"** and continued rowing upstream.

If something like a development backlog exists, there must also be something where ideas are created and perhaps even evaluated in one or more steps. Slowly, the entire process started to unfold in front of us. "Look, this is how it works here", began one of the team members. "There is a **Product Backlog** where more or less all product requests are collected. Before something lands in our Development Backlog, we must first analyze the individual requests in order to know how and when we will deal with it."

Several other team members started to clear off the space on the left side of the board because one column after another was being added. In the meantime, one glance was enough and they started telling me everything that was happening upstream. It looked more or less like this:

- First, product ideas were collected in an **idea pool.**

- These ideas were roughly sorted during a **triage** (a preliminary selection).

- **Business case** rough drafts were created for the selected ideas.

- The business case rough draft then went to the **Steering Committee,** who decided whether or not an idea should be followed.

- Once the Steering Committee approved the rough draft, a **detailed business case** was created.

- The detailed business case again needed to get final approval from a **committee.**

Phew! The **entire value stream** had grown a bit (please take a deep breath and turn the page).

47

The team was quiet. **"Okay, that doesn't look very agile"**, someone commented. Exactly. Of all the things in this entire process, the burden was placed on the development teams to become faster. The development teams could only attempt to catch up a bit of the time that was being wasted in the entire process. And there was a lot of wasted time.

The pre-selection triage was held monthly—that sounded relatively fast. The Steering Committee, however, only met **four times per year** and decisions on the detailed concepts only happened **once a year.** It took an **eternity** for an idea to get through this decision-making process before it landed in the Development Backlog.

Essentially, before something could be developed, there was a months-long (and often even years-long) pre-process that consisted mostly of waiting. Put another way: Flow efficiency—the ratio between **working time and waiting time** — was in trouble. Yet management expected a faster Time-to-Market by focusing on making a small portion — namely in the development teams — agile. **Business agility** is **not** created when teams hold their Daily Standups and search for improvements during their Team Retrospectives. That is at best (local) agile development, which is okay.

However, it has nothing, **ABSOLUTELY NOTHING,** to do with **business agility.** And business agility will never be achieved if all of the slow-moving process and system logic is simply maintained without consideration for the end-to-end system. Despite these agile development practices, this organization remained a lame duck. **End-to-end management** of the value stream was missing.

> **Business agility is created through lean processes that rapidly implement ideas, thus allowing teams to be able to deliver something quickly.**

What is Flow Efficiency?

*Flow **Efficiency** denotes the proportion of time where **active work** is being done within the total cycle time for a piece of work.*

CAUSE #4:
WIP LIMITS AT THE WRONG PLACE

Working on too many things at the same time is one of the **biggest afflictions** in organizations—work is not limited. As mentioned, many people in this company had spent time delving into agile methods and principles, including limiting the Work in Process (WIP). WIP limits are generally associated with **Kanban,** denoted as numbers at the top of individual columns showing the maximum amount of work allowed in the system at any given time. Almost all the teams in this company that used Kanban worked with **WIP-limited systems.**

There is also an "implicit" WIP limit in **Scrum.** It comes from working in Sprints and the associated Commitment to a certain amount of work that should be completed in the Sprint. During a Sprint, no additional work is allowed to be pushed into the system, thus defining more or less a maximum **WIP per Sprint.** The effect of implicit or explicit WIP limits is, among other things, that the **cycle times decrease** and the **predictability** of work completion increases.

The good thing was that almost all teams in this company worked with explicit or implicit WIP limits. Unfortunately, it didn't seem to help. So, were the WIP limits just wishful thinking, or was something else going on here?

But first, let's take a short detour and delve a little deeper into WIP limits.

Why do I use "Work in Process"?

If you are already familiar with Kanban or agile methods, you might be asking why it's called "Work in Process" here. You're right, originally the Kanban community had agreed upon **"Work in Progress",** *which was good since the term "process" has a negative connotation in many organizations.*

For me personally, **"process"** *is a neutral word because it should simply describe how work is performed in an organization. The problem in many companies is they have a lot of work in process that doesn't make any progress. It's at a standstill, so to speak. That's why I started using "Work in Process" consistently because it better describes the reality within the organization.*

HOW WIP LIMITS WORK, WHY THEY WORK AND THE ADVANTAGES THEY BRING

In a company, visualizing work is a **good first step** towards improvement. However, you must also understand and discern what this visualization shows you in order to undertake the right actions. Obviously, you can see what is being worked on, who is working on what and where there are problems. When I visit a company for the first time, however, in many cases I see that there is **too much work in the system.**

Let's imagine a system in which ten employees are working on 200 things at the same time. It would look some-thing like the next illustration. The board is covered with 200 notes and a second board might be necessary to hold all of them. The point is that this visualization is misleading. It would lead you to believe that ten employees are actually working on all these things. Unfortunately, the reality is that nobody is working on most of the 200 items in the system. That means there is a lot of "Work in Process", but not much **"Progress"** — very little work advances although it rolls around in the system.

The implication is that you cannot determine when work will be finished in a system running at capacity (congested). Predictability and adherence to delivery schedules are not present in such systems!

People are **not** capable of multitasking because **true multitasking** would mean that you could fully concentrate on doing two separate tasks at the same time. Could you work on two completely independent tasks on two laptops—like writing a different story with each hand? Probably not. And even if you could, at some point you would run out of body parts that could be used to complete additional tasks. When we think we are multitasking, what we are really doing is **"task switching"**. We continuously switch from one task to another; we set aside one piece of (unfinished) work and no one else works on it in the meantime.

Ready	A	B	C	Done
Active Work	Doing 📄	Doing 📄	Doing 📄	📄📄
Inactive Work	Waiting	Waiting	Waiting	

Back to our **board:** If an employee works on **20 different things** on average, you can assume that they are rarely concentrating on one specific piece of work. Most of the time, a little bit is completed on one piece of work and 19 other pieces of work remain unfinished. Since it isn't just one employee working this way, but ten employees doing this, 190 pieces of work out of 200 are left sitting. That can be illustrated on the board quite easily. In the upper part of the board, only the tasks actively being worked on are displayed. In the lower part of the board, the inactive work at that point in time is displayed.

Visualizing the work shows the true dysfunctionality of a system. The real way to improve things is by limiting the amount of work that is allowed into the system.

53

HIGHER FLOW EFFICIENCY – FASTER SYSTEM

The ratio of active to inactive work in the system can be measured. By calculating the **flow efficiency,** we can make assertions about how much of the cycle time is actually active working time.

Let's assume that the cycle time for a piece of work is ten days. Translated to our board, the flow efficiency details how many days a piece of work spends in the active part and how many days in the inactive part. Shockingly, the flow efficiency in most organizations is **very low.** With "low" I mean under ten percent, i.e. only ten percent of the "cycle time" is active working time.

The flow efficiency is primarily influenced by two factors:

1. **How large** is the portion of the value creation chain you can see? The larger the portion, the lower the flow efficiency will be. We just have to think about the extensive value stream of this company we are looking at (see Cause #3). The decision-making process used to determine whether or not an idea will be implemented already slows down the active work immensely. A little work is done and then they have to wait on a decision, which can sometimes take several months.

2. **How much work** is in the system? The more work that is rolling around in a system, the flow efficiency is guaranteed to be worse. There is a difference if you are constantly jumping between three pieces of work versus ten pieces of work.

This means that the **Work in Process** has a large influence on the flow efficiency. If an organization wants to **become faster,** the primary focus should not be on optimizing the active work. That is exactly the **problem with many efficiency programs:** They focus solely on the active work and want to make it faster. Let's assume a flow efficiency of ten percent, and you drive the people to work twice as fast. You can still only gain a maximum of five percent in system performance because 90 percent of the time, the work is inactive. Attempting to improve individual performance doesn't move us forward. It makes more sense to **focus on the system** and work on improving the performance there.

If the motto is "Be faster!", the consequence should be that there is less inactive work in the system, i.e. the Work in Process must be reduced.

54

REDUCING WIP: PARK THE WORK IN FRONT OF THE SYSTEM

That's all well and good, reducing WIP... but how should it be done? Does it mean declining orders? Let me put your mind at ease. No, it doesn't mean declining customer orders. The work must be kept in **front of the system** by using an Option Pool, for example.

What should be the **advantage** of doing this? Before, the work was waiting in the "Inactive Work" area and now in an Option Pool. What's the difference?

For the following **thought experiment,** let's assume that there is only one person working on the tasks and this person is never impeded. Let's suppose that there are three tasks — **A, B and C** — in our Option Pool in front of the system. Each task requires **five weeks** for the implementation. If we work with a **WIP limit of 1,** we must decide which task we will start with: A, B or C. Let's work on the tasks in order. We select A and are able to fully concentrate on it (B and C remain in the Option Pool).

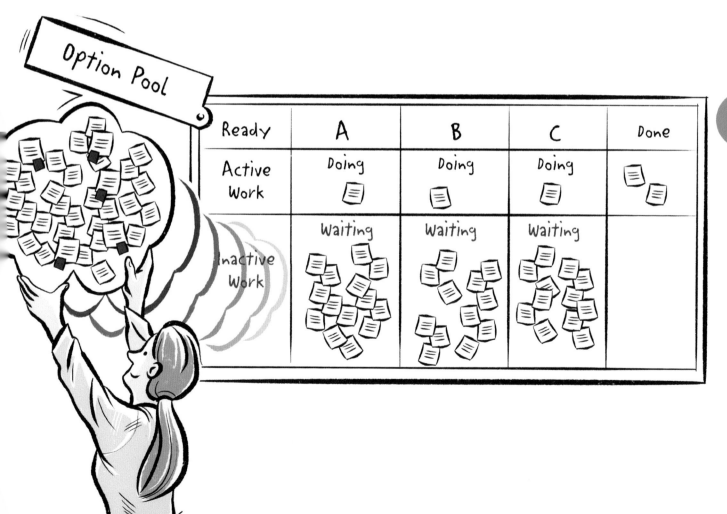

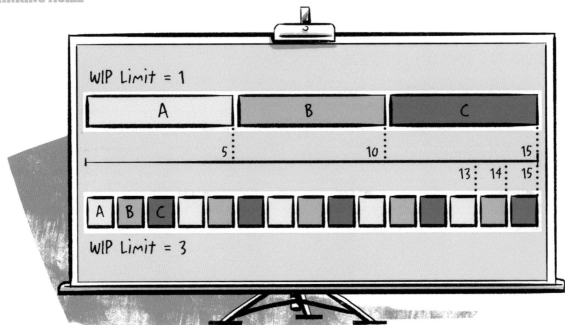

Task A is completed **in five weeks.** After A, we start work on B and are again able to completely focus in it — **task B** is finished after the **tenth week.** Finally, task C is worked on. Since we are able to focus solely on **C,** it is completed after the **15th week.**

Let's increase the **WIP limit to 3** in a new thought experiment and start working on **all** three tasks at the same time. We have come to the realization that people are **not** capable of multitasking. So, the person switches between tasks A, B and C, working on each task for one week at a time. In this variation, task **A** is completed after the **13th** week, **B after the 14th** week and **C** after the **15th** week. Now we see the difference.

With a **WIP limit of 3**, all three tasks have a high cycle time. With a WIP limit of 1, **some** tasks have a high cycle time.

Let's compare:

A: 13 vs. 5 – an incredible improvement in performance!

B: 14 vs. 10 – also not a bad improvement

C: 15 vs. 15 – remained the same

The point is, nobody says that all work in a WIP-limited system will be completed lightning fast (and if someone says this to you, forget they said it). The fact is that customer A will be served **faster** than customer B, and customer C has to wait a bit longer. However, you can **predict** when customer C will be served.

Strangely enough, I often get to hear the argument, "But that's **unfair!**" Which more or less translates to, "It's better if we serve all customers equally poorly." Do I need to say more, or can I just leave it at that?

Of course, I have presented the differences with over-simplified assumptions. Clearly, this doesn't mean that only one task should be worked on at a time. I am not using this example to say that 1 is the optimal WIP limit! But, a **WIP limit of 10** is **better** than a WIP limit of 100. In addition, permanently switching between tasks is not free—there is an enormous overhead that goes along with it. Even if you don't take the additional overhead into account, it is still clear: **Less WIP means shorter cycle times.**

You don't have to believe me, because thanks to **John D. C. Little,** this has been mathematically proven (Little & Graves, 2008). According to **"Little's Law",** the average cycle time of a system in which new work is always entering is the average number of tasks in the system divided by the average throughput.

It's about finding the right limit for the given system through continuous observation and allowing work to enter the system in an economically suitable sequence.

$$\text{Avg. Cycle Time} = \frac{\text{Avg. WIP}}{\text{Avg. Throughput}}$$

- Cycle time: the amount of time a task spends in the system
- WIP: the number of tasks in the system
- Throughput: the number of tasks completed in a given timeframe

If you have ten tasks hanging on the board and five tasks are completed each day, the average cycle time is two days. If you have one hundred tasks hanging on the board and five tasks are completed each day, the average cycle time is 20 days.

Life can be really simple sometimes—if we let it be.

John D.C. Little

57

A Quick Recap: Why I think WIP Limits are Really Good

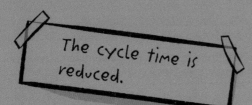

The cycle time is reduced.

The **cycle time is reduced.**

If we have fewer things to work on at the same time, the stuff we are working on will be finished faster. In the example with tasks A, B and C, the average cycle time for a WIP limit of 1 is ten weeks. With a WIP limit of 3, the average cycle time is 14 weeks. The cycle time is directly connected to the time-to-market. If you want to improve the time-to-market, you cannot avoid limiting the Work in Process.

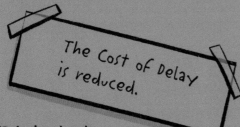

The Cost of Delay is reduced.

The **Cost of Delay is reduced.**

In the first scenario of the ABC example, we already made money on task A in five weeks because it was completed. In the second scenario, it took 13 weeks. The time difference of 8 weeks is the Cost of Delay. If we were able to make 10,000 Euros per week with the completed task A, we would have lost 80,000 Euros of revenue in the scenario where the WIP limit was 3. This is a fundamental point: WIP limits have an **economic component!**

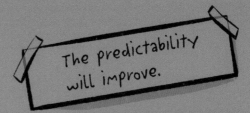

The predictability will improve.

The **predictability will improve.**

If several tasks are worked on in parallel, you lose the overview of how long each individual task actually needs. By thinking about parallel tasks, time buffers are calculated in so that the work gets done on schedule. WIP limits improve the **focus** on fewer tasks and help to understand how much time will actually be needed for a task.

The delivery risk is reduced.

The **delivery risk is reduced.**

Projects are often bound to deadlines. Let's assume that you agreed to deliver all three tasks—A, B and C—by week 13. In the scenario where **WIP=1,** A is delivered after five weeks and B after ten; there isn't enough time to finish task C, but the majority of it is there. In the WIP=3 scenario, neither A nor B are ready by week 13, and by no means can C be delivered. In reality, shortly before the delivery date in week 13, panic sets in and everything is done to at least deliver something — even if the quality of work is poor. A lower WIP limit takes the **pressure off** because work can be **continuously** delivered.

They reduce expensive multitasking or task switching.

They reduce expensive multitasking or **task switching.** WIP limits prevent too much work from being started all at once so the focus remains on what is really important and needs to be completed right now. Along with this, WIP limits reduce the associated overhead costs caused by task switching. Thus, WIP limits make a system more **efficient.**

WIP LIMITS— LARGE IMPACT IN THE FINE PRINT

The fact that 99 percent of companies do not **completely** think out their WIP limits strategy certainly has something to do with the history of methods like Kanban or Scrum. For a long time, Kanban and Scrum were basically seen and marketed as **high-speed plug-ins for teams.** So WIP limits became instruments to limit the amount of work in the teams so that the teams would be faster. Fundamentally, this is okay if these teams only work for themselves and are not part of a larger context.

However, teams are usually part of a larger organizational context, which means that the topic of WIP limits should also be understood in this larger context.

If the overall company performance — the business agility – should improve, you must read the **fine print** on how to use WIP limits.

So, let me **magnify** the fine print for you:

You must limit the work where you want the effect, the value and the benefits of WIP limits to be realized.

59

So, now our company works on initiatives—the agile term for projects. What happened with these initiatives once they had been chosen?

The overall initiative idea was first split into **partial aspects,** i.e. Epics, which are estimated units of work, the sum of which should result in the final product. A hypothetical example of this would be (for illustrative purposes only):

The initiative is **"World Domination".**

One Epic from this initiative could be called **"Conquer Germany".**

In order to be able to implement an **Epic,** there are other smaller steps necessary. So, the Epic is broken down into the next smaller unit, the so-called **User Stories,** that describe the individual **functionality** that is desired.

Because this individual functionality is created through various small pieces of work, User Stories are split into **Tasks.** These are pieces of work that can be completed within a day, for example.

That is how it worked in this company. In other companies, it could look completely different, where perhaps projects are split into work packages, and work packages into tasks. What's important is simply this fundamental message: **Extensive work tasks,** such as projects, are not completed in their entirety at a single desk, but are instead broken down into **logical subunits of work.**

Where did this company want to see the positive effects of WIP limits? Actually, they wanted to improve the time-to-market for the initiatives.

Then what needs to be limited?

Bingo! The initiatives.

So, now let's examine what actually happened in this organization. **Responsibility** for the company's agility was primarily placed on the teams. The teams were the ones **limiting** their work — the Stories and Tasks — while more and more projects were being pushed into the system from above. Agile teams often lead management to the false conclusion that even more projects can be started because theoretically everything must go faster. That's why it was impossible for these teams to improve anything on the time-to-market because an essential factor influencing it — **the number of projects in the system** — had not changed.

You can imagine this to be like an **interstate** at 100 percent capacity. The roads (= teams) are equipped with the most modern traffic systems and high-tech road materials enabling you to drive really fast. But you don't get very far on a plugged-up interstate, even if you would be able to drive 100 mph. You can be happy when you move forward at a snail's pace and you can't predict at all when you will get to your destination. It also doesn't help to constantly yell at the other drivers to drive faster.

So, it shouldn't surprise anyone that the time-to-market didn't improve. The units that have an effect on the time-to-market, i.e. the initiatives, were absolutely not limited. If the team level has no influence on the time-to-market, which part of the organization does?

Again, bingo! The strategic portfolio management.

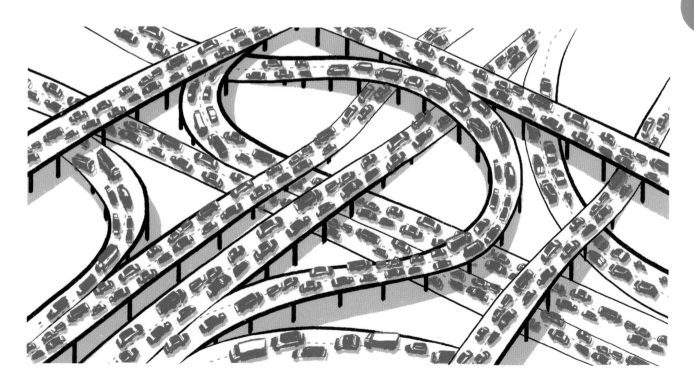

WHAT IS THE PROBLEM WHEN STRATEGIC PORTFOLIO MANAGEMENT IS MISSING?

Strategic portfolio management is the part of an organization that decides which initiatives will be implemented when. While there was an incredible amount of change undertaken at the team level, there was an incredible amount that stayed the same within the rest of the organization. There were several overloaded Excel documents discussed again and again in the various prioritization rounds, and actual agile strategic portfolio management didn't exist. My hypothesis was: Because **strategic portfolio management** was missing, too many initiatives were being started in this company.

I would like to take another **example** from my consulting work to explain the problems that occur when there is no strategic portfolio management. I had setup an enormous portfolio board together with the executive committee of a large corporation on five whiteboards lined up one after the other. While looking at the boards, we were discussing how they would like to operate in the future. "Now I finally understand what this thing should be!" one of the executive managers—let's call her Karin—blurted out in the middle of the discussion. Everyone looked at her in complete silence. "How does it normally work?", she continued. "For me it's like this: I have a 30-minute Monday morning meeting planned. Somebody who has been preparing for this meeting for a week comes in and presents an idea to me. They are really enthusiastic and, as I listen, I have to agree that it is a great idea. We absolutely must implement the initiative because it secures our future. On Tuesday, another person comes to me to present an idea that they have been working on for two weeks—this time it takes only 15 minutes. **Again,** I think the idea is great and we must implement it. And on Wednesday, **another meeting.**"

Her point was: In these pitches, there is a lot of preliminary work invested and an understandable desire to get the initiative approved. And these ideas are probably also really good.

But what happens? Basically, Karin makes three individual, **isolated decisions** on Monday, Tuesday and Wednesday. She is missing the **overall context** of all current and planned initiatives.

By describing this, Karin really pinpointed the problem. **Executive management** makes decisions every day about whether or not projects will be started. They not only make these decisions **isolated** from their executive management colleagues, as well as from all others in the company who must implement the project — they make decisions without considering all the other projects currently being implemented.

Isolated individual decisions continuously increased the WIP of the initiatives—despite the initiatives needing to be limited.

63

NO SPACE FOR PICKING UP

Let's return from our excursion into the world of WIP and get back to our company.

I wanted to test my hypothesis, **"too many initiatives started"**. So, I asked for an appointment with management. At this appointment, I asked how many initiatives were completed each week.

How can that information be determined? In the case of this company, it was quite simple: Every initiative was tagged with a start date and a completion date. First, I sorted the initiatives according to their weekly completion date and cumulatively recorded them in a diagram (denoted by the **"finished"** line).

That looked pretty **good.** The line was consistently going upwards, which meant that initiatives were actually being completed.

You can do the same with the **start dates.** Again, I sorted the initiatives according to week, recorded the cumulative results in the diagram with a second line, **"started".** This line also went upwards—except that isn't good in this case.

Why was I not happy?

When I drew in the average throughput of the system, i.e. the average "departure rate" of initiatives (lower red line), everything seemed more or less okay—work was being completed. Doing the same thing with the average start, or "arrival rate" of initiatives, the line created had a much steeper gradient. This was a clear sign that **more initiatives were being started than were being completed.** If the number of employees is not increased by at least a proportional amount, which was the case here, it is cause for concern.

I knowingly and gladly use the terms **"arrival rate"** and **"departure rate"** in this context because this situation always reminds me of an airport. If you imagine an airport, it's obvious that if the **arrival rate** of airplanes is higher than the **departure rate** of airplanes over a longer amount of time, a huge problem is created. If the gates and runways are parked full with airplanes, at some point **nothing can move.**

65

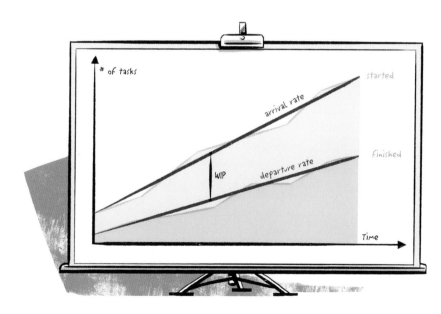

If **too many projects** are started within an **organization,** at some point nothing is moving. Obviously, when more is done, the company can make more money—that is a reasonable conclusion. However, this conclusion hasn't been completely thought out. The imbalance between starting and completing work can only be maintained for a certain amount of time. When the next airplane lands, i.e. one project too many gets started, the entire system starts to fall apart and there is more work "in process" than can ever be completed.

Money cannot be made with incomplete projects and eventually customers become annoyed waiting for their products. That is what happened in this company. Because they spread themselves too thin by starting too many initiatives, they undermined their position in the market and with their customers.

WIP limits are a way to align **arrival and departure rates,** i.e. start and completion rates. They help to ensure that there are not more projects started than can be completed in the time a company needs to remain viable.

There was a remarkable improvement recommendation given at the end of this executive management workshop. Thinking out loud, one of the mangers said, "In the future, instead of holding our assessment rounds in isolation in our meeting rooms, let's meet in front of a **board with all the currently running and planned initiatives.** That way, we can see how the newly pitched ideas fit into what is already in progress and what is already planned. And whether or not it even **fits.** Do we have to immediately start the initiative because it is such a great idea, and stop something else being worked on, or does it first go into an idea pool?"

Do we need WIP limits?

In many organizations, if the topic of **WIP limits** comes into play, management automatically poses the question about which projects should be stopped or not implemented at all. But that's not the point. WIP limits should not prevent projects; they should support decisions that make business sense. Such as what should be delivered next in order to fulfill the business interests of the company and create value for the customer? This requires a change of thinking because in most organizations they like hearing the sentence, "Yeah, we're working on it" This sentence makes me nervous. Employees shouldn't be permanently working, they should be delivering. **Working costs money, delivering makes money.**

Despite all of the difficulties, this company was already quite advanced in the way they were thinking. Even if the **WIP limits** *were used in the wrong place until now, there was always an awareness that* **work** *in the system must be* **limited***. Many organizations do not make this leap in thinking and believe they can manage without WIP limits just fine.*

Whether or not WIP limits are needed *can be easily tested. You can do a quick check:*

☐ **Everyone, ourselves as well as our customers, is happy with the performance of the organization.**
Congratulations! Everything is in order and you have already found your optimal WIP.

☐ **Everything is moving too slow. The customers are complaining and the business figures are cause for concern.**
In order to gain speed, you should reduce the WIP.

☐ **We are delivering to the market faster than our customers are able to buy our products.**
That is a nice problem to have—you can start more work.

67

A FIRST ASSESSMENT

Let's summarize why the desired effects were not achieved in this company. Management had many **good intentions** with their **change initiative** and were exemplary in their examination of the topic of agility. They tried to internalize the mindset behind the methods and, in doing so, slowly but steadily advanced the organizational culture development. However, in their excitement to get started, they failed to deal with the mechanics and dependencies within the company first. Instead, they tried to implement agility with a classical project management approach. But an essential question remained unanswered: **Which changes have an effect and why?**

Because the word **"agile"** automatically seems to include the word **"team"**, the greatest **point of leverage** for what they wanted to achieve at this point was left completely unexamined. It wasn't going to be found at the **team level.** There were four serious causes for why they did not get closer to, and in some cases were further away from, their primary goal of **"better time-to-market":**

Change and agility were seen as issues for the teams rather than for the entire organization.

Nobody was managing the dependencies between the teams.

There was no end-to-end management of the value creation chain.

There was no strategic portfolio management.

68

SO THAT'S WHAT WENT WRONG IN THIS COMPANY

PART 3

The Solution

It's flying,
it's flying
...an
improvement

About **product** boards,
strategy boards and the desire
for **collaboration** across all
Flight Levels.

We certainly had not identified all of the problems. In my view, however, we had identified the one with the greatest impact—namely those that prevented the company from making the first big step towards **actual** improvement.

I don't only get contacted for assistance when an agile transition is on the brink of failure. Often, I will be included in the planning phase of such change projects, and I introduce the **Flight Levels** model right at the start.

As the name says, Flight Level describes **how high** an airplane is flying. Depending on the flight altitude, the degree of detail you observe the ground below will change. If you are flying at a very high altitude, you can see for miles in the distance but at the same time you cannot see every detail on the ground. On the other hand, if you are flying at a lower altitude, you can almost look into the bedroom window, so to speak. However, you can no longer recognize the areal extent of the city.

Each flight level has its own characteristics and **advantages** but also has **limitations** on what can be seen.

We can use the **same principle** in organizations. Using the Flight Level model, we can find out which level of the organization offers the best **leverage for improvement.** It isn't important which methods are used at each level. Instead, it is more important how the **communication and cooperation** is set up between the Flight Levels and between the various departments within each level. If you can make improvements here, the entire value creation will start being optimized—and that is ultimately **our goal.**

The Flight Level model is a communication instrument to identify the effect of specific improvements at the various levels within the organization and to discover where within the organization it makes sense and/or is possible to leverage improvements.

73

FLIGHT LEVEL 1: OPERATIONAL LEVEL

Let's start **closest** to the ground. The first Flight Level belongs to the teams that complete the daily work. A team can optimize themselves, or better said can optimize their individual workflow by implementing **four essential actions:**

- They **visualize** their work.

- They use **WIP-Limits.**

- They integrate routine **feedback loops** such as measurements, Daily Standups or Retrospectives in their process.

- They determine **improvements** through these feedback loops and implement them.

The **method** a team uses to develop a product or provide a service—agile or whatever—is completely irrelevant because the Flight Level model works **independently** of any particular method. There is often more than one team in a company and each team has a preferred way of working. That's why you will come across **various** Flight Level 1 systems within an organization.

In order to generate **value for the customer,** these individual systems typically must cooperate in some fashion—**no team is an island.** If you ignore this fact and place your focus only on optimizing individual teams, the risk of suboptimization arises. Yes, you will have a high-performing team. However, the overall **performance** of the organization, i.e. the combined performance of all teams, remains the same in the best case, but will most likely **decrease.**

74

visualizing the work

setting WIP limits

establishing feedback loops
(measurements, Standups, Retros, etc.)

determining and implementing improvements

Welcome to the world of system thinking! Local optimization often leads to global sub-optimization (see the keyboard example in Part 2). The reason for this is the **dependencies** between teams: There will always be some dependencies that cannot be resolved. These dependencies need to managed—that is the responsibility of **Flight Level 2.**

FLIGHT LEVEL 2: COORDINATION

Teams make their contribution at various places in the value stream—one in development, another in marketing and a third in the operations area. The trick is getting the right team to work on the right thing at the right time. Thus, with **Flight Level 2,** we zoom out from the team level in order to visualize the **value stream,** which is the way particular product is created (assembled from pieces) or service is fulfilled.

The focus at Flight Level 2 is on the coordination of end-to-end, from idea to reality, value-generating activities. At Flight Level 2, the interactions between teams are optimized.

Important: Flight Level 1 and Flight Level 2 must **communicate** with one another. That's why at Flight Level 2, in terms of optimizing collaboration in a value stream, we use the same that are used at the team level:

● The work will be **visualized.**

● **WIP limits** will be utilized.

● There are routine **feedback loops,** such as Standups and Retrospectives with the team representatives.

● **Improvements** are derived and implemented from what is learned in the **feedback loops.**

Since workflow is optimized across the entire value stream, waiting times at the interfaces are reduced. And most importantly, **bottlenecks** become clearly **visible.**

The larger the organization, the more value streams there are in the form of various products and services. Thus, you will typically see **more than one** Flight Level 2 system in a company, and so there are dependencies existing between the various value streams. If, for example, something is changed in a product, often something will also need to be modified in a different product. In such cases, the various boards used to manage the value streams are combined at a single location in order to make **dependencies visible** and manageable. Feedback loops are also established here for coordination purposes and to catalyze improvements. What is created is something like **operational portfolio management,** which is also the responsibility of Flight Level 2.

FLIGHT LEVEL 3: STRATEGIC PORTFOLIO MANAGEMENT

A company's **portfolio** is normally comprised of a number of products and services, as well as strategic initiatives that should make the company fit for the future. This mix is managed at **Flight Level 3.** You want to gain an **overview** of everything happening within the company. You want to know which services and strategic initiatives are influenced in what way, how far the implementation has come and whether a product, service or initiative pays off strategically and is as **successful** as you hoped. Can a new project already be started or should you wait until another one has been completed? At **Flight Level 3,** one of the most important questions to be answered is:

How much work can be sustained in the organization and is the work aligned with the strategy?

The **overview** at Flight Level 3 makes the strategic management of the entire organization possible. It isn't meant to micro-manage operational implementation. Fundamentally, having more demand than you are able to fulfill is a good problem to have, otherwise a company must reduce its workforce. Because of this, however, competition between the options occurs at the strategic portfolio level. Disparity between the urgency of each **option and the implementation** possibilities needs to be clearly stated, otherwise there might be an impression that an endless amount of resources is available. This is not the case, though, and this is exactly what Flight Level 3 deals with. At this flight level, it's going about wisely **choosing and combining** strategic initiatives, projects and products to be developed, recognizing dependencies and **optimizing** flow through the value creation chain based on the actual resources available.

You also work with visualization at the **strategic level,** in this case by using a **Strategy Board.** The design depends on the organization—"standardized" Strategy Boards don't or shouldn't exist (unless your strategy is "We want to be a bad copy of company XY"). The larger the organization, the more systems there will be at Flight Level 3. These can be at various locations or in various divisions of the company. It is recommended, however, that the overall **company strategy** and supporting strategies, such as those from the various locations, are clearly visible on the Flight Level 3 board. In the best case, these strategies are connected to any **key figures** that will indicate if things are moving in the right direction or not.

And now a request from the inventor: Please do **not** use the Flight Level model to restructure your company or divide it up into Flight Levels (à la "We want the Spotify model")!

The Flight Level model is neither an organizational model nor a maturity model—Flight Level 3 is not three times better or more important than Flight Level 1.

The Flight Levels are a tool to help you **think and communicate** and should simply make you aware at which **level** (and not in a hierarchical sense) leverage is available for solving a problem. Each Flight Level has a different focus:

● At **Flight Level 3,** the focus is on prioritizing upcoming projects and initiatives according to the **strategic direction** of the company.

● At **Flight Level 2,** the focus is on **breaking down** the chosen projects and initiatives into actionable pieces and **coordinating** the work with the participating operational units.

● At **Flight Level 1,** the teams involved in the **operational work** separate the tasks of the project/initiative into smaller packets and are focused on **delivering** them.

The Flight Levels simply visualize and organize the various types of work within a company. Strategic decisions must be made on what will be developed, then the implementation must be coordinated and finally delivered. At the same time, an organization might prefer to make strategic decisions based on closer contact with the coordination level rather than from their ivory tower. Perhaps Flight Level 3 and Flight Level 2 fuse together onto one board. There are as many configuration possibilities as there are companies.

It also isn't necessary to involve all of the Flight Levels for every project. Something that only affects a team within the company and can be resolved within the team, such as correcting a small quality issue, doesn't really have a place on the strategy board. On the other hand, far-reaching strategies, like better time-to-market, cannot be implemented if all of the responsibility is handed over to the individual teams. A single development team would probably not be deciding whether a particular product will be developed or that a new manufacturing plant will be built in China as a precautionary measure. If you want to make an improvement in an organization, you must first be clear about **which level** has the greatest amount of **leverage** for achieving it. The Flight Levels should help **identify** the correct level. Generally speaking, it can be said that:

The higher the Flight Level, the greater the leveraging effect.

If the possibility exists to start an **agile transformation** at Flight Level 3, you should do it. Because the only agile team that you absolutely need at the beginning of an agile transformation or change initiative is an agile upper-management team that practices agile strategic portfolio management. Everything else follows from here—**lead by example.**

If you need to make changes in an **existing system** because it has run into trouble, you should first look where you have the **fastest** access. Experience has shown that the fastest access is often at Flight Level 2. And this is exactly where we **started** in our faltering company.

IMPROVEMENT 1: MAKE DEPENDENCIES VISIBLE AND MANAGE THEM

During the **problem analysis,** the team realized that there were more dependencies on one another than they were aware of when setting up the team boards. However, there will also be several teams working together on a product in the future, thus the dependencies will persist. Let's recall the mess of dependencies that had taken over between the teams in product development.

It was important to me that those involved understood one thing: **Value for the customer** is only created when they receive the right product. The customer doesn't care how the people working on and delivering the product were organized and structured. It doesn't matter if they are unhappy with the product or completely satisfied with the product. They only care about the value created for **them.** That's why a structural reorganization should not be the beginning of an agile change initiative.

Business agility is achieved when delivering value to the customer is optimized. Sooner or later, it becomes clear what needs to change in the organizational structure to support this.

83

MANAGING DEPENDENCIES BETWEEN TEAMS: DEVELOPING PRODUCT BOARDS

One thing should be clear: It will never be possible to have absolutely no dependencies between teams, services and products within an organization. However, you can and should make it a habit to eliminate dependencies whenever possible. For example, sipgate, a highly innovative and profitable German telecommunications company, envisions themselves becoming a company without dependencies [Mois & Baldauf, 2016]. Everyone understands this vision might never be completely achieved, but they see it as a **continuous task.**

If dependencies cannot be eliminated, you must manage them. How can you get a handle on managing these dependencies?

As a first step in this company, we simply found out which teams were involved in the development of each product. There was no need to be a master detective for this since the organization was setup along product lines. Depending on how many teams there were per product and how large the teams were, we either held workshops with everyone involved or team delegates took part in setting up the **product boards.**

Visualizing. First of all, those involved with each product thought about how it was developed, how the teams collaborated in the development process and at which points in the process, as well as in which direction, dependencies existed. For each product, this process was visualized on a **product board.** For smaller teams, we found out that this visualization could replace the **team board** because there was much more useful information, often with much better quality, on the product board. At the same time, the product board also gave them an overview of the broader context. From that point on, these teams held their team Standups and Retrospectives in front of the product board. In comparison, what I have observed in many other organizations is that larger teams often still need their own boards because there is a greater need for internal team coordination.

Limiting. If you want to achieve a faster time-to-market, for example, you must limit the units which have the greatest influence over it. At Flight Level 2, this means not starting more than you can finish. The team delegates took this message to heart and worked together to define the optimal amount of work for Flight Level 2.

Establishing feedback loops. A combined product board itself is not enough. The board doesn't affect much, it simply portrays a situation. That's why I advise against putting all the brainpower into visualizing and setting up buffers, swim lanes and impediments.

"Managing dependencies" means continuously examining what is on the board and coming to the right conclusions from what is portrayed. To quote Russell Ackoff once again: We need agile interactions. This requires communication in order to actively coordinate the flow of work through the system.

85

We need agile interactions. This requires communication; you must actively coordinate the flow of work through the system.

Russel L. Ackoff

Thus, appropriate **coordination points** were defined:

In the Product Standup Meeting, team delegates (in a rotation, for example) meet two times per week in front of the product board and coordinate the workflow through the system for the respective product at this level.

In the Replenishment Meeting, the delegates together decide which work enters the system next and, more importantly, how much work enters the system. The delegates take into consideration which internal and external people must be involved in order to achieve a suitable prioritization. By the way, if you are in a WIP-limited system, the principle of "Stop starting, start finishing" applies. This meeting is only held once other work has been completed—before that point, there is no need to replenish.

In cross-team Retrospectives, team delegates examine how the collaborative delivery of value has worked till now and whether something can be done to improve it. The Retrospective was chosen as the meeting format because those involved already had experience with it at the team level. This is an important point: In most organizations, Retrospectives are done exclusively at the team level, thus reinforcing local optimization.

Metrics are an ideal feedback loop and were already being utilized in this company. So, metrics were also introduced at the product level, which was a huge advantage because they are especially meaningful when used here. First, you are much closer to the customer at the product level. And second, the measurements already contain all the dependencies. Measurements at the team level always only represent how much work a team has completed in a given timeframe. However, if you use measurements like cycle time and throughput at Flight Level 2, you can say how much "product" was created within a certain timeframe, or how much of what you are producing can **actually** be sold.

More meetings?

Incidentally, **the point** of using product boards to manage dependencies is not the boards themselves. What's important is that the right people talk with each other about what they see on the board—this is the interaction we want. This seems like a flood of additional meetings since there are several products and several Flight Levels, thus multiplying the number of Standups, Replenishments and Retrospectives. Do you really need to torment people with more meetings? **Two remarks about this:**

● **Do you need to keep all the old meetings?**
I have seen corporate divisions with more than 2000 employees radically rid themselves of all their old meeting formats. Instead, there were only Standups, Replenishments and Retros. Other meetings were only held when there was a need for clarification beyond these three basic meetings.

● **Everyone does not need to participate.** Team delegates are sent to the Flight Level 2 (and also Flight Level 3) meetings since they are needed for rapid decision making. So, there are only a few individuals with additional appointments rather than all team members. These meetings are not regular meetings requiring several hours where participants present endless PowerPoint presentations. I'm talking about short, quick meetings that are done within 15 minutes—which is exactly why all essential decisions are made there.

With or without meetings, there is still a need for coordination. To avoid having meetings, you can certainly write thousands of Emails, or only a few teams coordinate with each other, or each team continues to make their own isolated decisions—but these are clumsy solutions that require **additional coordination** rather than bringing improvement.

87

MANAGING DEPENDENCIES BETWEEN PRODUCTS: OPERATIONAL PORTFOLIO MANAGEMENT

On the product boards, there was still an area called **"Waiting on External".** Compared to the parking spaces with the same name on the team boards, this one doesn't necessarily mean that we are waiting on another team to finish their part of the product. Dependencies between teams involved with developing the product were managed on the product board (Intra-product Dependencies). As you saw, these dependencies were greatly reduced through actively managing them.

"Waiting on External" means there is a dependency **outside** of the depicted product value stream, most often to a different product (Inter-product Dependencies). Whether at the team or product level, dependencies are inconvenient. How can you get control over the dependencies at the product level?

After we had setup the boards for the individual products, we took a closer look at which dependencies existed between the products. Then we filtered out products that had a lot of dependencies between them. I bet you can guess what we did next?

We thought about we could focus and improve the work in this value stream and followed our **familiar process** for this:

Visualizing. We detailed the working process for these products (the portfolio) on one board. By doing this, the dependencies between the products became internal dependencies. These dependencies didn't need to be depicted separately because they are actively managed by communicating through feedback mechanisms like Portfolio Standups. In operational portfolio management, external dependencies are those necessary connections and influences that are located outside of the product development, such as dependencies to suppliers.

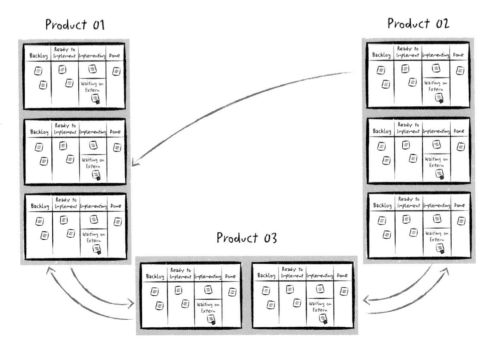

Limiting. Next, we made sure that there was an optimal amount of work in this system; at the Portfolio Level, for example, it is the number of Epics. Above all, the work should enter the system in a strategically relevant sequence based on agreed upon criteria. For me, one of the most important criteria for prioritization was the desired **outcome** a piece of work should deliver.

Establishing feedback loops. Again, feedback loops were set up in order to discuss what the product boards were showing. The dependencies were able to be managed, and necessities and possibilities for improvement could be identified. More specifically, the feedback loops were comprised of Portfolio Retrospectives and Portfolio Metrics. In operational portfolio management, for example, it is interesting to know how many days the cycle time is increased due to waiting on external dependencies. If value-oriented metrics are not already used at the team level, you should at least focus on measuring the economic outcome that is being delivered instead of how much is being delivered at the portfolio level. Ten features at 1000 Euro each or one feature for 10,000 Euro?

If you would put the all the boards for the individual products in one room, each board would have a column at the very left that is often labeled as **Backlog.** In this column, there is a stockpile of work that should be implemented for each product. Ideally, this work is put into an order of execution based on certain criteria, i.e. prioritized. When doing this, only the dependencies within the workflow of one product will be managed.

If we want to manage the dependencies between several products, it's a good idea to bring all the products together on a **single board** and, as a result, establish a **collective Backlog.**

What happens if each product has its own Backlog? If, for example, a piece of work for Product 3 is completed, the Product 3 team would pull the next piece of work and would continue working without taking into consideration the value streams of Product 1 and 2. Put another way: **What the others are doing is their problem.**

Backlog		Analyze	Implement	Acceptance	Delivery	Acceptance
📄 📄	Product 1	(2) 📄	(3) 📄	(3) 📄	📄	
📄 📄	Product 2	(1) 📄	(2) 📄	(4) 📄		
📄 📄 📄	Product 3	(2) 📄	(2) 📄	(3)		
		Waiting on External				
		📄 📄				

With a collective, **cross-product** Backlog, the rule that the next highest-priority piece of work should be pulled still applies. Now the following situation can occur: A piece of work for Product 3 is finished, but the next highest-priority piece of work in the collective Backlog belongs to Product 1 because it is more important based on business characteristics. The teams working on Product 3 would have nothing to do for a period of time.

The first question you should ask in this situation is: "Can we help out other teams?" Maybe it isn't possible because different technologies are used in the teams for instance. In this case, the **alternative** is that the "idle" team can work on improvements or other things they usually never have time to work on in the meantime.

If such situations seldom occur—that a product is ranked behind all other products for a period of time—there is no reason for concern. I would only take a closer look if this situation came up often. It could possibly indicate that the knowledge in the organization is distributed in a way that the business priorities cannot be optimally addressed. What we see is another example, at a higher level, of local sub-optimization vs. global optimization. If each product has its own Backlog, uneven knowledge distribution within the organization would not be noticeable. The product teams optimize their own area, which is not necessarily what is best for the entire organization.

The advantage of a collective Backlog when managing several products is that such **irregularities** are made visible. Then you are able to ask yourself whether the existing portfolio structure supports or hinders the company's success.

Whether you make the situation visible or not, your company is in this situation. I prefer to have the problems in front of me because only then can the brain focus on finding a solution.

In the case of this company, I wasn't able to get them to follow my recommendation to set up a collective Backlog—and that's also ok. However, the idea is waiting in the Idea Pool as a **future improvement.**

IMPROVEMENT 2: INTEGRATING THE UPSTREAM

Business agility is the ability of a company to adjust to changes in the market and the demands of their customers. If the company's solution for this is to simply make a department or even just a single team agile, they haven't understood the challenge. Of course, you can apply agile practices exclusively to product development or service delivery, but as we observed in this company, the effect is limited. When agile teams reach the borders of the non-agile portion of the organization, they will eventually get stuck and be unable to reach their goals. This might make placing the blame easier but isn't the least bit helpful to the company or its customers.

Because it is so pretty, I would like to once again show you a picture of the actual value stream of this company. By examining more closely what happened upstream, a review and approval process was established upstream, before the developers lifted a finger to work on something.

THE THREE UPSTREAM TIME TRAPS: TOO MUCH, TOO EXACT, TOO UNNECESSARY

The **upstream process** having a gazillion steps is itself nothing bad—if these steps could be completed quickly. In the case of our company, however, there was a several month waiting period between the board meetings where ideas were evaluated and assessed. In all probability, at some point these steps were implemented with the best of intentions and we didn't need to eliminate them completely.

Generally speaking, it's better to examine these types of preliminary processes and determine what is redundant and what could perhaps be shortened or merged. I came across three main problems when we scaled the value stream to include the upstream processes:

1. THE ANNUAL BUDGET CREATED BATCH SIZES THAT WERE TOO LARGE

In organizations, there is a big fight once a year about the budget, when management either waves through or rejects ideas based on the concepts presented. Collecting ideas over a longer period of time kills any bit of business agility, not to mention that real life pretty much never follows an annual plan. With an annual budget, your reaction time is once a year. Let's imagine this depicted on a portfolio level board: Every chosen option sitting in the Backlog moves to the "Committed" column on January 1st, thus it must be implemented. On January 1st, what needs to be delivered by December 31st has already been decided. And despite this, teams will still be tormented with pointless discussions about methods and requirements, such as "you must groom your backlogs, limit your WIP and work in Sprints". If what needs to be delivered has already been decided, the whole agile fairy dust is completely unnecessary and has absolutely no effect, especially in regards to business agility. That's why team agility has **nothing** to do with business agility.

When we talk about **business agility,** we are talking about the inner workings of the organization. Reaction time must be quicker and this starts with a new budgeting process—in other words, replenishment. For example, if you want to be able to take responsive action on a monthly basis, there should be a monthly replenishment interval. However, this doesn't mean starting something new every month! The same principles apply here: Work in progress must be finished and WIP limits must be considered during replenishment meetings. The trick is to make tasks small enough so they can be completed and put on the market as quickly as possible, thus creating value.

Look, the annual plan is finished.

Super, then we definitely know what we are not doing tomorrow.

ANNUAL PLAN

2. COLLEAGUES AS SUPPLIERS

Likewise, **business agility** often prevents positive relationships between various company departments. Similar to a supplier relationship, departments give "orders" to the in-house IT department and want to know to the penny how much it is going to cost. Determining the time and/or cost is a similarly protracted procedure of estimations, approval and new estimations, just like external order requests. The primary product from this process is very expensive paper because ultimately the estimates will most likely be incorrect. For me, the most vivid example comes from a financial institution: It took five days to estimate that it would take the IT department one day to implement a certain feature. Another classic: cost estimations. It costs 80,000 Euros to estimate that a feature would cost 30,000 Euros to implement. If the order is given, the department steps back, leaves the internal supplier to work on it by themselves and only becomes interested again when the product is delivered. This is anything but agile. Otherwise, it would be clear that within the same organization you actually work together on solutions for your **external customers.**

3. MAKING AN ESTIMATE FOR SOMETHING THAT MUST BE DONE ANYWAY

Not only are there estimation orgies for the things you want to do, but ironically also for those things you must do. A manager at a financial institution told me that according to their internal guidelines, they must estimate to the hundreds of Euros how much a certain piece of work would cost. "We have estimated 567,300 Euros", she told me proudly. I wasn't able to bite my tongue and asked if they would still do the implementation if it only cost 10,000 Euros or if it would cost 10 million Euros. "Of course, we have to implement it because it is a legal requirement!"

I am not saying that estimations are completely unnecessary. I do believe, though, that the effort for making estimations needs to be limited if the business should become agile. An estimation only needs to be as exact as necessary, not as exact as possible. In order to decide for or against an idea, you need nothing more than an approximate size of the implementation. Whether or not an idea has a future can only be determined if you show the customer something they can evaluate.

Wait a minute...

I want to explain this to you first!

Based on the upstream processes, Business Agility means:

that the Replenishments follow the pull principle, take the WIP limits into consideration and are done in a cycle appropriate that matches the desired level of business agility;

that an estimation on approximate project size is enough to get started;

that not only cost and effort are estimated, but above all the benefit as well as the revenue are also estimated;

that a concept uses as little paper as possible, instead creating actual results as quickly as possible;

that the customer is included as early as possible somewhere in the development process.

Based on the upstream processes, business agility means:

● that the **Replenishments** follow the pull principle, take the WIP limits into consideration and are done in a cycle that matches the desired level of business agility;

● that an **estimation** on approximate project size is enough to get started;

● that not only **cost and effort** are estimated, but benefit and revenue are also estimated;

● that a concept uses as **little paper** as possible, instead creating actual results **as quickly** as possible;

● that the **customer** is included as **early** as possible somewhere in the development process.

If you find out after a previously agreed upon timeframe that an idea is not going in the right direction—wonderful! If the opposite is true—also great! We didn't waste money on estimating and instead gained experience and developed a piece of product.

The question isn't how many steps are part of the upstream value stream, but instead how quickly these steps—from the first step to an assessable unit of value (idea, concept, etc.)—are able to be executed.

BETTER TIME-TO-MARKET THROUGH FREQUENT DECISION MAKING AND BETTER TEAMWORK

We had a discussion with the upstream colleagues—the business area. It was immediately clear to them how much valuable time was being eaten up in the decision-making process, so they were willing to simplify things. Up to this point, new ideas were pre-selected once a month. Business cases were then written for the selected ideas and either approved or rejected on a quarterly basis. Approval for the detailed concept only took place once a year.

Once again, I depicted the **pre-selection processes** on a board and discussed with the upstream delegates which of these processes were really necessary. After some back and forth, the business people decided that a rough concept was more than enough for them to decide whether an idea should be implemented or not. The goal of development itself was to include the business area more—by taking part in the Standup meetings, for instance. That way, action could be taken earlier if development on a piece of work was not going in the **right direction.**

From the original five upstream steps, only two remained in the end: "approximate business case" and "waiting on approval". We agreed that the approval or rejection of rough concepts could be done **every two weeks**—only if the WIP limits in development permitted it because other work was already completed. In my view, this was one of the most **important decisions** for making business agility a possibility for this company in the future.

97

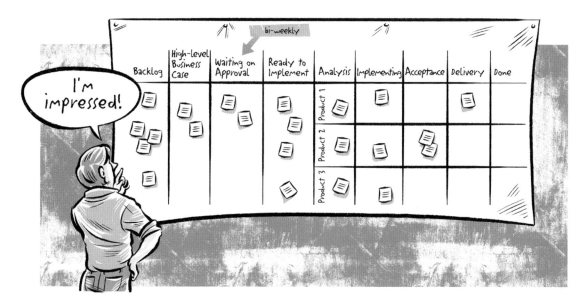

However, the **time factor** was only one aspect. Decision making in a two-week rhythm instead of once a year naturally has an immense influence on the time-to-market. But something much more important happened here: An integrated view of product development was created. There was no longer business here and development there. These two areas joined up and pulled together so the organization could survive and the customer could get what they really need more quickly in the future.

This **pulling together** was supported most of all through routine feedback loops setup between the business departments and product development:

- **Standup meetings** were held jointly with representatives from the business departments in front of the product boards.

- In addition, regular joint **Retrospectives** were held.

- **Metrics** were chosen to give an exact picture of how many projects and products, from idea to completion, were undertaken in the entire organization and how long it took.

Business agility means going from idea to delivering value to the customer as quickly as possible. This works when an organization is not split into groups of people giving orders and groups of people executing orders and instead gradually removes the demarcation between "us" and "them". Dealing with and overcoming dependencies on each other can help the organization become more cohesive.

Cross-functionality has nothing to do with team setup

It all sounds very romantic, doesn't it? The fact is, though, this is about enormous change. Why should the business departments simply go along with it?

The demarcation between "us" and "them" is a fundamental historical problem that exists in most organizations, regardless what type of organization it is. This can be attributed to specialized splinter groups that typically organize themselves into departments. They split themselves apart from each other and the whole organization. Requests and results are usually "given over" (or tossed over) to the other departments, whose approach and requirements might be completely different than in their own department. Then the demarcation can be seen: the departments are a red flag for product development, software developers are better than software testers, the business departments see everyone else simply as suppliers, and so on.

Trying to make a company agile does not inevitably make this situation better. Cross-functional teams are great to have and an important part of the company. However, it doesn't necessarily mean that old prejudices just disappear. Now you just have cross-functional Team A that performs better than cross-functional Team B. Instead of functional silos, there are cross-functional silos. Congratulations! If you reduce the dependencies and combine teams according to product lines, Product Y is naturally more idiotic than Product Z. And taken from the portfolio point of view, there are only complete morons sitting at the top. With "performance" bonuses, you can easily reinforce this animosity or even make it worse. In doing so, only individual parts of an organization will be optimized, but not the value creation for the customer.

This competition must first be removed. As I have shown with this company, it isn't as easy as it sounds. It is a cultural process that already starts with recruitment. The required maxim should be "don't hire skills, hire attitude". Sure, subject matter expertise is important, but it is much easier to acquire subject matter competence than it is to change attitudes. Cross-functional teams are in no way the Holy Grail of agility making social points of friction between the performance areas of a value stream just magically disappear—sometimes they just shift. Bringing together various schools of thought in one team is still better than focusing on individual performance or on the performance of individual specialist silos. When it's about focusing on the customer, integrated value generation is only a small drop in a very large bucket.

Cross-functionality is a company mentality and not an organizational setup for teams. It means creating an environment where it is ok, or even desired, to perform poorly locally (whilst learning) if it helps the overall performance of the organization. It isn't enough having everyone is pulling on the same rope—they must all pull in the same direction, too.

IMPROVEMENT 3: STRATEGIC PORTFOLIO MANAGEMENT

Business agility doesn't work if an organization is comprised of **agile islands** while the logic of the surrounding processes remains the same and certain groups exempt themselves from practicing agility. Business agility starts **at the top** because executive management is still responsible for the strategic direction in most organizations. In the agile scene, many believe that organizations must manage without any hierarchy. I also think that many organizations are too hierarchical, but I do not believe that it can work without any management whatsoever. The decision to "work without a hierarchy" has to be decided by someone—presumably it isn't the building maintenance person making this decision.

Getting **executive management** on board is not always easy, however. The expensive MBA knowledge is deeply anchored in their minds. But an agile company doesn't need a business administrator at the top, it needs a business leader. If executive management participation flounders, it's usually due to a lack of ability and willingness for critical reflection. Many top managers live—often unwanted—in continuing education celibacy. Part of the reason for this is that top managers—but different than top athletes—are in constant competition and don't take time for training, i.e. acquiring new abilities for competing. In many cases, I can also understand this. Managers are constantly running from one appointment to the next, they are completely overbooked and are pressured from all sides. Nonetheless, they must be the pilots on the agile journey to avoid just sinking money into the local sub-optimization hole.

Out of this grows the **illusion** of being able to react quickly to the market—and yet, annual budget cycles are still followed. What should and will happen over the next year is determined from the perspective of a certain point in time. Ultimately, you unleash an enormous amount of money, creating a project wave that should distribute itself into calm rivers continually rolling out new ideas and products. In nature, mountainous waves do nothing more than destroy everything as they travel inland. Within an organization, this creates an exhausting cycle: When the wave recedes, many people are left sitting around twiddling their thumbs waiting for the next mountainous wave. The main thing is that everyone knows when the year starts what they certainly won't be working on in the afternoon of August 17th. Namely, what is stated in the annual plan.

Real business agility integrates the upstream and the downstream into a single value stream to create a fast and steady workflow. Put another way: Strategy, operations, development and delivery closely work together and, most importantly, towards the same goal. For this to function properly, executive management must be on board.

103

HOW DOES STRATEGIC PORTFOLIO MANAGEMENT WORK?

The reason was clear why the time-to-market in our company didn't work out as planned. While development teams followed all the rules and limited their work with blood, sweat and tears, the strategic level continued to start one initiative after the other. And that is exactly what happens in many companies wanting to become agile. This approach creates two conditions: confusion and stress. Let's recall:

You must limit the work where the effects, the benefits and the advantages of WIP limits want to be seen.

In an organizational system, the **ratio between** initiatives that have been started to those that have been completed has a direct effect on the time-to-market. Strategic portfolio management is responsible for keeping this ratio in the correct balance and aligning these initiatives to the overall strategy. In order to align the work in the entire organization to the strategy, upper management must be willing to unequivocally and explicitly communicate the strategy and all the current initiatives within the organization to the employees. Just like with the other Flight Levels, I also use the three familiar steps with upper management to get their strategic portfolio management on track:

1. **Visualize.** All value-generating units currently in the organization are depicted on a collective board. At Flight Level 3, these are primarily projects and initiatives. We also determine how these projects will be executed. According to which criteria are project ideas assessed? What follows the strategy and what doesn't? What does the selection and decision-making process look like and when is an initiative considered successful? Where do the ideas and recommendations for initiatives come from and what is being worked on and where within the company?

2. **Limit.** In the second step, the optimal number of value-generating projects that the organization can handle is determined. At the strategy level, "value-generating project" means when the project or initiative is completed and lands in the last column on the board, you would ideally be able to see what result was achieved in the market. You can only start new projects when projects or initiatives are completed according to this requirement— and if the WIP allows it.

3. **Establish feedback loops.** If the entire organization should be aligned towards the strategy, delegates from every level must be integrated into the cycle, from making decisions to measuring success. They are all included in Standups and Retrospectives. And just like at all other levels, the same principle applies to strategic portfolio management: Dabbing at the strategy board one time is not enough. The trick is to find possibilities for improvement and take the necessary action. And this doesn't mean improving the board, it means improving the work at the strategy level.

The specific design of these steps can, must and should look different for every company. And the design can change over time based on the needs of the company and its customers.

THE STRATEGY BOARD

At this point, I'm going to say it one more time: This is not the **strategy board** that can be used in every company in this world or across the universe. I am showing the strategy board used within the specific context of this company.

You are allowed to be inspired, but copying is strictly forbidden.

Let's first look at the left side of the strategy board which I built together with the upper management of this company. Quite clearly to the very left, company strategy was concisely written down and in the next column the business metric were broken down. For example, if the strategy states that the market share in Asia should be increased, the corresponding metric "Market Share Asia" must be able to depict these changes. From this point on, the project and initiative tickets running across this board would include which strategic business metric should be influenced by them. This way, strategic alignment of the organization is achieved. It's not only clear to everyone what is being worked on, but also why something is being worked on.

The principles for building a **strategy level board** are the same as at the other levels. First, we identify what type of work is done in strategic portfolio management. Second, we ask ourselves how this work is to be completed.

Together with upper management, we identified **two types of work:**

- **Initiatives** were the organization's money makers; essentially, the products and solutions for the customers.

- **Investments** denoted necessary, but not urgent, projects that didn't have a direct benefit for the customer, but had a background affect. As a Netflix customer, for example, you purchase problem-free video streaming and not automated software testing. But to deliver this product, Netflix needs to setup the appropriate infrastructure for it.

Finally, we depicted the steps that individual work types must go through on the board. The most fascinating piece was at the right side of the board. Let me interrupt for a second: The primary difference between operative and strategic portfolio management is the timeframe. In the operational area, everything revolves around what is being implemented now, whereas strategy also deals with what happens in the future. Naturally, this is a huge challenge since the future is sometimes full of contradictions. What should you bet on? On something that brings money in right now or on projects that perhaps only show their benefit years later? Such considerations must be taken into account in strategic portfolio management. Thus, this level deals with **outcome** rather than **output.**

In strategic portfolio management, it's going about outcome instead of output.

On most of the boards in this world, you will usually find after a column that is labelled "In Development" a column tersely labelled as "Finished" or "Done". In this company, though, they saw it a bit differently. A project or initiative would only be considered "Finished" if it had achieved what it was supposed to achieve. And in order to determine this, metrics must be employed and feedback from the customers and users of a product must be gathered. It's possible that adjustments are necessary after receiving feedback. That's why this company had three additional columns after development on the strategy board: "Measure & Improve Success", "Adjust & Improve" and "Result (not) Achieved".

Where did the ideas for projects and initiatives, the "money makers", come from in this company? For the most part, these ideas came from the teams because they are closest to the customers and know better than anyone what the customer wants. Thus, the rough business cases were already evaluated by the teams to determine what could be achieved or which business metrics could be turned by implementing an idea. The business case also had to consider market response so a decision could be made within 90 days whether or not the desired result was going to be achievable. The idea didn't need to completely implemented within 90 days, but it should be possible to see the trend towards success after 90 days. These rough business cases were placed in the "Pool of Evaluated Ideas" and everyone submitting ideas came together every two weeks to discuss the strategic fit of each idea with their colleagues.

FEEDBACK LOOPS IN STRATEGIC PORTFOLIO MANAGEMENT

The meeting formats in strategic portfolio management are the same as those at the other levels. The Strategic Portfolio Standup is where updates are given on the progress of the projects and initiatives, as well as where action needs to be taken. Delegates from Flight Levels 1 and 2 pass information up to the strategy level and then carry the decisions made regarding the strategy back into the organization—this is how a **continuous strategic alignment** occurs.

In this company, **upper management** took part in the Standups along with delegates from the operative portfolio management at Flight Level 2. It was planned to have these meetings every two months, but things didn't go as planned already at the first Standup. There was so much information on the board that one of the managers immediately blurted out: "Every two months makes no sense!" I could only agree with that statement. Nonetheless, my statement regarding annual budgets in the meetings till now astonished everyone: "I think you should meet at least once a week. Better would be **twice a week.** Even after this wave has been worked through."

You might be asking yourself **why** such a short cadence? **The Strategic Portfolio Standup** is a meeting in which decisions will be (should be) made exactly when they are needed. Let's not forget what happened when managers made isolated decisions (see Part 2). There were more projects started than the organization could handle. The greater the time period between Strategy Standups, the greater the risk of falling back into old habits. Even if you would meet on a monthly basis, there is a high probability that a week later an urgent decision is needed for something else—and then the temptation arises to not wait for the next Standup. And if you would wait, that would be anything but agile.

I recommend holding Strategic Portfolio Standups on a weekly basis in order to make necessary decisions in a timely manner and in the context of the projects currently running.

110

Important meetings should be held frequently

People in organizations like to complain about meetings, which is partly due to how they are set up. But I also take a close look at how often important meetings are actually held. Most likely, you will find that the meeting intervals are too long (also making the meetings longer). The decisions made in these meetings lose value because people are forced to make permanent (isolated) decisions in the meantime.

Retrospectives at the strategic portfolio management level are also meant to improve collaboration. It allows those people working with the strategy board, namely upper management and delegates from Flight Levels 1 and 2, to regularly review what has occurred over a given timeframe. We agreed that the Retrospectives should take place once a month. As an attentive reader, you certainly have noticed that I think Retrospectives at all levels of the organization are extremely beneficial. Cliff Hazel from Spotify, in an interview I did with him, stated that if he could introduce only one thing into a company, it would be **Retrospectives**. They are the motor for a learning—and thus agile—organization.

And finally, we decided for a regular **Strategy Review.** Finding out whether or not the right things are being done is more important at the Strategy Level than any other level. The organization should not waste time on things that go nowhere. The focus of the Review was answering questions on how the market position and the market itself had changed, how the competition was behaving and if the strategy needed to be corrected in light of these changes. To start, we agreed on a **quarterly interval** for the Strategy Review.

As with many other points in this book, I would ask you to not simply copy these meeting intervals, regardless at which Flight Level. There is no general rule that applies to all cases, but I can give you the following **guideline:**

It makes sense to hold the individual meetings and workshops more often at the beginning and then get a feeling for the frequency that best fits your situation. Also, don't make the meetings fill up the entire evening—we are talking about meetings taking about 15 minutes when they are held twice weekly, for instance.

The company is on its way. Whether or not they will reach the goals they have set really depends on how great the temptation is to fall back into old behaviors and ways of thinking. **Together** with the dedicated people in the transition team, we were at least able to establish the essential requirements to **achieving their goals.**

No management of team interactions

No end-to-end management of the value creation chain

No strategic portfolio management

We built product boards to manage the dependencies within products

We scaled the operative product portfolio to include the upstream, simplifies the upstream and with it improved the collaboration between the departments and development

We established an operative portfolio management to manage the dependencies between products

We developed strategy boards with upper management to get an overview of all current and planned projects in the organization, enabling collective rather than isolated decision making in short cycles.

113

Naturally, there were still things that could be improved within this company. But my work was done for now. Since we were able to establish the most important improvements at the highest Flight Level, I was confident this company could continue on by themselves. The message had been received:

BUSINESS AGILITY IS NOT A TEAM SPORT— IT IS A COMPANY SPORT!

PART 4

The Result

What was the result after all of this?

About goals finally **being achieved**, gratifying business metrics and a journey that **never ends.**

116

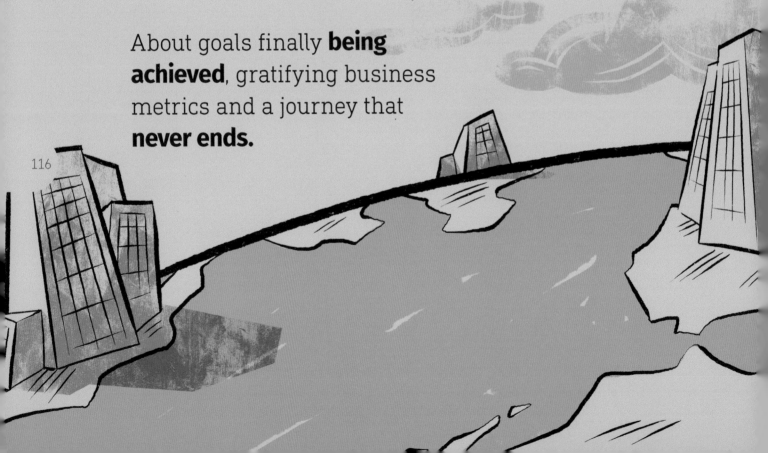

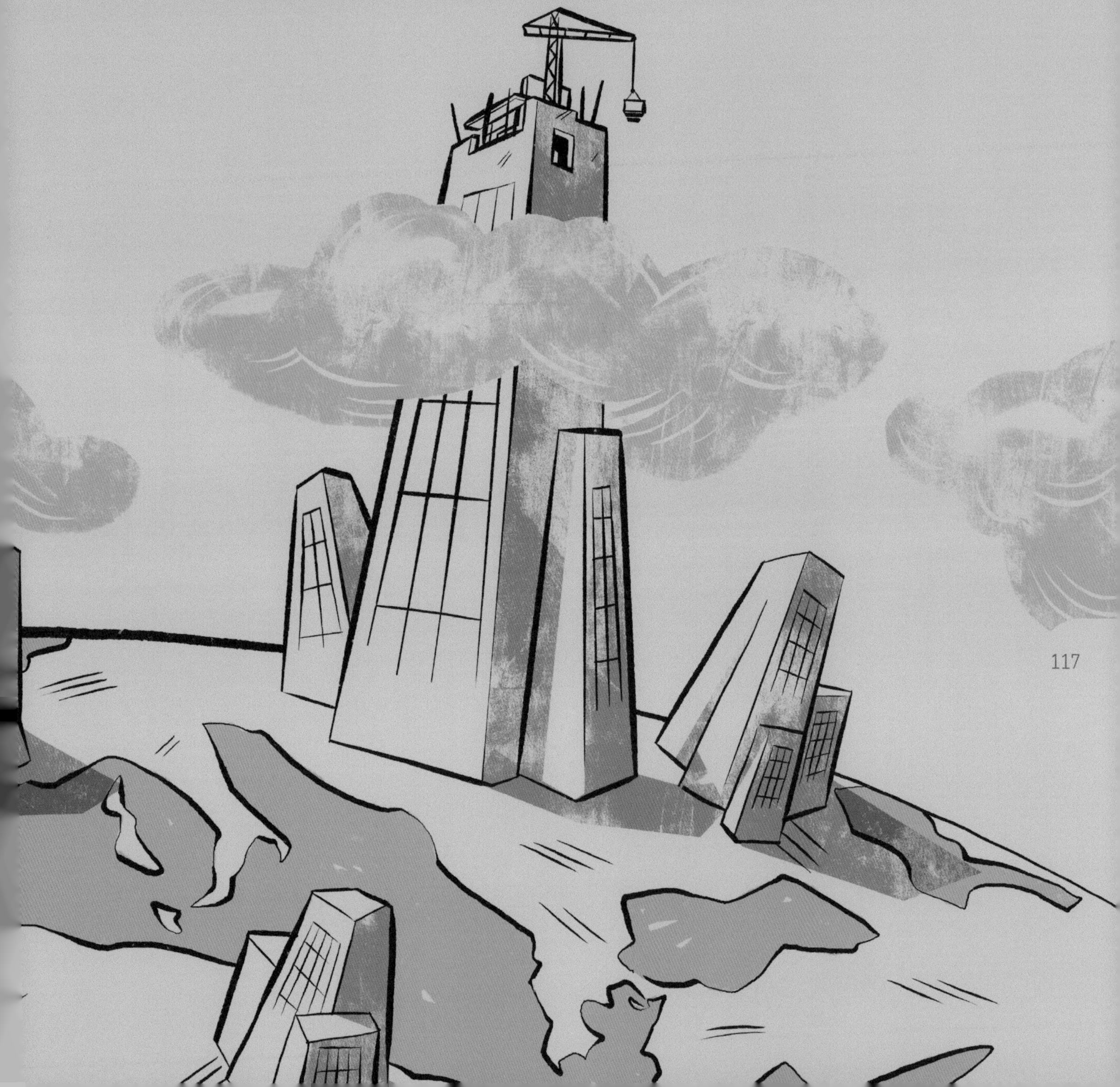

Even though I belong to the category of **"business consultant"**, it's always a pleasure when I am able to make myself redundant. There are basically two situations where I get called in to help. It is either before a company takes their first steps towards more business agility or after they have traveled long on the road to agility by themselves and start to stumble. In both cases, there is usually contact with the company even after my preliminary work has been completed. For instance, I see employees from these companies at conferences and they update me on how things have progressed. Sometimes they ask my thoughts on other actions they are planning or later on invite me to an **improvement workshop.**

So was the case with this company, too. After we established the essential steps, which you have read about in this book, the employees and the management continued the work for the most part on their own. They understood what was required for business agility and what mechanisms were needed to achieve it. When problems came up, they didn't resort to reactionary agile. Instead, they first examined the cause and tried to understand the correlation. This helped them find an appropriate solution for the company rather than using a cookie-cutter solution. Months after my work there, the employees I spoke with told me that a profound cultural change had been put into motion within the company. They said: "We have achieved so much, but we now know that we will never be finished. The development **will always continue."**

Three years after we put their unsuccessful transformation attempt back on track, management invited me to see the company's development since then. I was very pleased with what I heard.

TIME-TO-MARKET REDUCED! YAY!

Being faster on the market had been the primary goal for the company, which they struggled to achieve. Now, three years later, things finally looked different. On average, initiatives were being completed seven months faster—more than twice as fast as before. The faster time-to-market goal also put many other things in motion and, because of this, it became clear what else needed to change in order to achieve this goal. The positive side effect: Closer examination of the weaknesses that were revealed brought **massive improvements** in other areas.

AN INNOVATION LEADER ONCE AGAIN

Three years ago, there were signs that this established company would simply be catapulted out of the market by Startups with greater **innovative power.** After we built the **strategy board,** someone came up with a simple and effective idea during one of the regular improvement meetings. Using a color code, every new initiative was clearly labeled based on if the outcome would help differentiate the company from its competitors or if it would just get them to the same level as their competition as quickly as possible. The ratio of innovations to "me-too" products was initially anything but reassuring. **Three factors** started to change this ratio:

119

1. **Faster decision making.** One of the first actions undertaken was to radically shorten the miserably long decision-making process which needed to be completed before the IT people could start working. Good ideas no longer sit around for months. Now, taking into account WIP limits and strategic direction, ideas are passed on more quickly to development. To do this, it was necessary to replace cumbersome decision making during a few committee days each year with continual, frequent Standups utilizing the transparency of the Strategy Board. Standups have become second nature for everyone and management can more easily maintain an overview.

2. **Courage to experiment.** The company now trusted itself to simply try things out instead of over-specifying every new idea. This was one of the most difficult exercises for those in the company because failure goes along with experimentation. To admit to yourself and others that something didn't work was a cultural challenge. Upper management first needed to accept that failure is also a form of success if you take time to examine it and learn something from it.

3. **Faster Feedback.** Since the time-to-market has been radically reduced, user feedback for a product is received much faster than before, making it possible to make product changes using the lessons learned from this continuous feedback loop.

By the way, using feedback loops across Flight Levels and making quicker strategic decisions created a new cultural process in the company. Before, the company was a conglomeration of **silos.** The business silos isolated their innovation in a sluggish, centrally-controlled process and then pushed the work towards the IT silos where implementation occurred. IT was forced into the role of a mere supplier—a cost center.

Today, innovation comes from the entire organization, including the IT employees. Management finally realized that product developers are close to the market and their understanding of development is especially valuable. As before, certain decisions are still made centrally, but the process leading up to the decision making is no longer centrally managed. The employees feel that management listens to them and again understand why they are doing what they are doing.

STRATEGIC ALIGNMENT

Awareness of and individual's effectiveness within the company is reinforced by the portfolio management since all initiatives are consistently aligned to the strategy. The clearly formulated company strategy is still hanging at the left on the Strategy Board and is broken down into defined business metrics. The business metric being used to measure the work is noted on the tickets for each piece of work that wander through the company during development, and thus past the employee working on it. The employees involved in the development can see what they are able to achieve. Because of this, an environment of focus and bringing everyone on board has been created. The majority of employees understand where the company is heading and respond accordingly.

GREATER EFFICIENCY

At the beginning of its transformation process, the company found out the hard way that business agility cannot work if only a part of the organization takes responsibility for it. However, areas of responsibility outside of product development—such as Controlling, HR or Procurement—follow completely different rules. Although product development is for the most part a complex process, administrative tasks are often complicated [Snowden, Boone 2007 and Stacey 2000]. In the last four years, the administrative areas were also aligned towards agile interactions by using WIP limits and feedback loops. The focus here was much more on efficiency. Available employee capacity and slack time created by utilizing WIP limits was and is purposely used to automate and continuously improve routine processes with simple methods like Kamishibai (see below).

What is Kamishibai?

Kamishibai is actually a Japanese narrative theater which uses picture cards. In the Toyota production system, a visualization technique for recurring processes was developed based on Kamishibai. According to a process rhythm, tasks to be completed are written on cards and **visualized** in daily, weekly or monthly columns on a **board.** The type of tasks is written on the **front side** of the card and how the task should be done is written on the **back side** of the card. Once a task is completed, the card is simply placed in the **"Done"** column. Kamishibai serves as a mini-audit: Those working on the tasks are required to follow the processes, thus stabilizing them. At the same time, they also have an eye out for possibilities to improve the processes. Process improvement is no longer the job of a single auditor, but of every employee [Leanability E018, 2017].

All in all, this brought more stability and a more relaxed work environment within the organization. At times, though, this was a double-edged sword. Employees, who before were a fire-fighting task force heroically saving projects and processes, fell into the role of routine employee and that didn't sit well with them. This affected the employee structure. Whoever wanted was allowed to move to a different department and continue developing their skills, others simply left. Being so efficient that employees leave the company because of it sounds like a problem anyone would be happy to have—however, it's still a problem. For the routine processes, people who are comfortable doing this routine work are hired. This change presented a challenge for some time, but it was an important and very effective transformation.

FOCUS ON OUTCOME RATHER THAN OUTPUT

If you want an agile business, you should focus on the result and its effect, i.e. the outcome, rather than on the quantity, i.e. the output. In our company today, agility is no longer seen as delivering the largest quantity of initiatives as possible. Instead, more emphasis is placed on considering beforehand—even by the employees recommending ideas—what and how much an initiative contributes most and where the focus should be placed. A single initiative can create more value than three others combined; just making this assessment is already an important step. To a certain degree, it is difficult to measure the effects of this approach on the revenues and earnings performance. However, the fact is that the revenues have increased and it can be assumed that the **"focus on outcome"** piece of the puzzle also contributed to this.

COMPANY FINANCIAL FIGURES TREND

Yes, the figures. Did the entire agile effort pay off? Let me pull out four key figures for you.

● At some point during the transformation, the company came to conclusion that it would make sense to quantify the **Cost of Delay.** Put another way, they worked to determine the financial impact on the company if a product was released on the market earlier or later. Their calculations showed that the faster **time-to-market** had saved around ten million Euros per year in delay costs. When products arrive on the market seven months earlier, revenues also roll in seven months earlier. It's that simple.

● Which brings us to **revenue.** Despite the existing difficulties, the company's revenue growth always lagged at around two to four percent even before the agile transformation. In the last two years, however, revenues have greatly increased, with last year's growth approximately twenty-five percent (a 6 to 12- fold improvement).

● Over the last three years, **profit** has increased three-fold. This was due to higher revenues, as well as to lower costs thanks to greater efficiency.

● The **market capitalization** was more than doubled: from 3.4 billion Euros to 7.1 billion Euros.

Are these increases only attributable to the business agility that eventually took root? It would be too trivial to make this claim. Naturally, the right strategic decisions must always be made. I can say, though, these actions that were taken had a significant role in the company's success.

LET'S SUMMARIZE: HOW CAN YOU MAKE YOUR BUSINESS AGILE?

The story that has been told here should inspire you. Perhaps your company is in the middle of a transformation process and you find yourself confronted with one problem or another again. My hope is that I have been able to put you back on track towards solving your problems. Maybe your company is ready to start a transformation process and you realize that one or more of the previous considerations could lead your company in the wrong direction. Whatever your situation is at the moment, I want to summarize one more time what you need to pay attention to if your company's goal is to achieve business agility.

DISCLAIMER: This is not an exhaustive list and has no particular order. Some steps must be done more than once.

START AT THE TOP

The first agile team to be established should be upper management. And when I say agile, I mean agile. There has to be more than just lip service and generously delegating responsibility for the transformation to the lower hierarchy—"You have our blessing, go forth and become agile! It doesn't have anything to do with us." When I arrive at a company to help them get out of a rut in their agile transformation they are currently stuck in, managers are often very proud to show me their visualization abilities. "We have a task board which we use to track our management tasks. Next, we will work on the tickets 'Create Annual Budget' and 'Check Employee Utilization'." Congratulations on the fantastic to-do list with Post-Its,

but not everything you stick a Post-It on is agile. The job of upper management is to really consider what business agility means, which problems need to be dealt with and above all what their role is in this process.

AGILITY BEGINS WITH THE CHANGE PROCESS

You cannot implement new ways of **working and thinking** on schedule. All of the successful transformation projects I have seen till now already experienced during the transformation process itself what they ultimately wanted to achieve. Should an organization practice the pull principle? Then the employees must also be allowed to "pull" the changes. Should teams make incremental deliveries? Then don't write a two-year transformation plan. Changing from push to pull means finding allies, marketing the idea and **getting everyone invested** in delivering customer value faster.

FOCUS ON THE GOAL, NOT ON THE METHOD

During World War II, the population of Melanesia saw the American soldiers coming from the sky as gods who brought wonderful things with them. There were no more cargo deliveries after the Americans withdrew, so the island's inhabitants began imitating the activities they had seen the soldiers perform on the airfield. They hoped they could get the gods to return. This is the story behind the term "cargo cult". In some companies, "Agile" is turned into a type of cargo cult. **The methods are worshipped, but not the goal.** It doesn't matter at all if a Standup takes 5 minutes or 20 minutes. Do you want to make your business agile or do you want to simply implement agile methods in your company?

AGILITY IS NOT A TEAM AFFAIR

If you want an agile business, your focus should be on generating value (organizational processes) and not on organizational structure. Clearly, you need teams for the processes to work. But it makes little sense to optimize teams come hell or high water because optimal teams encompassed by broader bad processes contributes very little to business agility. From a systemic point of view, it is much more **effective** to have great processes with bad teams.

IDENTIFY THE FLIGHT LEVELS

Since business agility is not a team affair, you should identify which Flight Level in your organization will be able to address which problem. Should initiatives be completed more quickly? Then the number of initiatives must be limited rather than optimizing teams. What must be done along the entire value creation chain, from idea to result, in order to maximize the effects? Comprehensive thinking means upper management must absolutely be on board. Otherwise, you will eventually hit a **glass ceiling** and will go no further.

127

MANAGE AND ELIMINATE DEPENDENCIES (EXACTLY IN THIS ORDER)

You must get used to the fact that there will always be dependencies within an organization, regardless how it is structured. And I use the words "always" and "never" very sparingly. So, let me repeat myself: There is no use in copying the magical structure of a different company, even if it seems like the right solution. A better approach is to make your interactions agile. Eventually, any dependencies that impede the workflow will become visible and you will be able to deliberately decide how you can reduce or eliminate them.

INCORPORATE THE DRIVERS FOR LEAN BUSINESS AGILITY AT EVERY FLIGHT LEVEL

Let's assume you have identified the various Flight Levels within your company. Regardless if a team, product or strategy board will be built, the following four steps should be incorporated at every flight level:

1. **Make the work and the processes explicit.** Most of the time, knowledge work is invisible and, as such, difficult to understand. On a board, you can see what is being worked on and how it is being worked on. However, it is essential to depict the existing processes and not the required or desired processes. Progress is best achieved when you start with the status quo.

2. **Consciously manage WIP.** WIP limits are one of the most powerful management tools available. They influence many variables whose interactions result in business agility—for example, time-to-market or

predictability. This doesn't inevitably mean WIP limits need to be reduced. Setting WIP limits means understanding which WIP impacts what. And sometimes this means increasing a WIP limit again or simply leaving it as it is (see the questionnaire at the end of Part 2).

3. **Frequent feedback loops.** Nobody wants to make a company agile just because there is nothing better to do. Agile transformations pursue specific goals, so it is extremely helpful to know where you are at right now. You need regular feedback from experiences. Metrics can clearly show if an action had an effect or not. You can then decide accordingly to do more or less of something, or discontinue doing something completely. Another classic feedback loop is talking with each other. One of the greatest discoveries of humankind is speech. You are welcome to try this out. In a business context, it is even more brilliant to talk to the right people about the right topics at the right time. This is exactly what creates agile interactions and this is what I have been emphasizing throughout this book.

4. **Improve.** Everything you have done in the first three steps still only gives you the latest state of error. So, don't invest too much energy in trying to find the perfect visualizations, perfect WIPs and perfect meetings on your first try and then keep them that way forever and ever. There is no such thing as the absolute right whatever, only something that works right now. The trick behind business agility is improvement. Therefore, start doing as soon as possible, reflect on what you are doing and improve upon it.

128

REFERENCES

[Laloux 2016]
Laloux, Frederic: Reinventing Organizations:
An Illustrated Invitation to Join the Conversation on
Next-Stage Organizations. Nelson Parker 2016.

[Leanability E020, 2017]
Leanability Videoblog: Lean Business Agility E020 –
The Spotify Model.
https://bit.ly/2OOILjM

[Leopold 2016]
Leopold, Klaus: Practical Kanban: From Team Focus to
Creating Value. LEANability PRESS 2016.

[Little, Graves, 2008]
Little, John D.C.; Graves, Stephen C.: Little's Law. In:
Chhajed, Dilip; Lowe, Timothy J. (eds.): Building Intuition.
Insights from Basic Operations Management Models
and Principles. Springer US 2008, p. 81-100.

[Snowden, Boone, 2007]
Snowden, David J.; Boone, Mary E.: A Leaders's Framework
for Decision Making. In: Harvard Business Review,
November 2007.
https://hbr.org/2007/11/a-leaders-framework-for-decision-making

[Stacey 2000]
Stacey, Ralph D.: Strategic Management & Organisational
Dynamics. The Challenge of Complexity. 3rd edition,
Financial Times 2000.

[The W. Edwards Deming Institute 2018]
The W. Edwards Deming Institute: Quotes by W. Edwards
Deming.
http://quotes.deming.org/authors/W._Edwards_Deming/quote/10141

LITERATURE TIPPS

Selected Articles on the Topic of Business Agility

My thoughts on the Topic of Business Agility are captured on my blog. You can read it at
www.LEANability.com

New interviews with Business Agility practitioners can be found regularly on my video blog at
www.LEANability.com

Flight Levels

At which Flight Level does innovation start?
http://bit.ly/2DYXzJy

Lean Business Agility E007: Flight Level 2 at AutoScout 24
https://bit.ly/2IXke9z

Lean Business Agility E026: Medical Device Development, Flight Levels und Scrum
https://bit.ly/2QRj4PJ

Podcast: Flying at Portfolio Level
https://bit.ly/2CLzAxW

WIP-Limits

WIP Limits Must Die
https://bit.ly/2E9nFdP

Flow Exercise: Building Paper Boats
http://bit.ly/2waOHuU

Book Recommendations

Christensen, Clayton M.: Competing Against Luck. The Story of Innovation and Customer Choice. Harper Business 2016.

Doerr, John: Measure What Matters. OKRs – The Simple Idea that Drives 10x Growth. Portfolio Penguin 2018.

Goldratt, Eliyahu M.: The Goal. A Process of Ongoing Improvement. North River PR Inc 2014.

Kaltenecker, Siegfried: Self-Organising Enterprises. Leanpub 2017.

Liker, Jeffrey: The Toyota Way to Lean Leadership. Achieving and Sustaining Excellence through Leadership Development.

Marquet, L. David: Turn The Ship Around! A True Story of Building Leaders by Breaking the Rules. Portfolio Penguin 2015.

Moore, Geoffrey A.: Escape Velocity. Free Your Company's Future from the Pull of the Past. Harper Business 2011.

Reinertsen, Donald G.: The Principles of Product Development Flow. Second Generation Lean Product Development. Celeritas Pub 2009.

Ries, Eric: The Lean Startup. How Constant Innovation Creates Radically Successful Businesses. Portfolio Penguin 2011.

Taleb, Nassim Nicholas: Antifragile: Things that Gain from Disorder. Penguin 2013.

Practical Kanban
From Team Focus To Creating Value
Klaus Leopold

LEANability Press
1. Edition 11/2017 – revised translation of
"Kanban in der Praxis"
353 pages, also available as kindle and on leanpub
as EPUB, Mobi und PDF
ISBN: 978-3-903-20500-0

Kanban Change Leadership
Creating a Culture of Continuous Improvement
Klaus Leopold

John Wiley & Sons Inc
1. Edition 04/2015 – translation of "Kanban in der IT"
304 pages, also available as kindle
ISBN: 978-1119019701

Printed in Germany
by Amazon Distribution
GmbH, Leipzig

17123993R00077